Me and My Magical Life

A Memoir

By:
Charlotte Plantz

Charlotte Plantz

Published by: Pajarito Graphics
Email: pajaritographics@gmail.com

ISBN-9781081708122

Cover art: **Collage -**
"Gwendolyn The Cowboy Plays Frisbee With The Moon"
by: Charlotte Plantz

Type setting and graphic design:
Mike Plantz

Dedication

This book is dedicated to all those who dream of a better life. And to those who find the courage to make it happen. My husband, daughters and grandsons: Mike, Julie, Cyndi, Andrew, Tyler and Alex are proof that it is possible.

Table of Contents

Dedication...i

Introduction...v

Preface...vii

1 Vision..1

2Murray..9

3 A Plan From Out of the Blue................................21

4 ChaconSummer...31

5 A Cast of Characters..41

6 The dinner Party and The End of a Magic Summer......49

7 Highlands University Student..............................59

8 The Anniversary Mass......................................65

9 The Christmas Gift...75

10 One-Way Ticket to Mexico................................81

11 Visit to Humboldt County.................................95

12 Mexico, Here I Come......................................105

13 Living a Creative Life As a Single Woman............119

14 Home for the Holidays....................................129

15 Memorable Christmas on the North Coast............135

16 Three Long Months..145

17The Wedding...157

18 The Next Two Years.......................................165

19 422 Second Street...175

20 My California Arts Council Career.......................191

21 Women in Management....................................203

22 Promotional Arts...217

23 A Family Worth Remembering...........................227

24 The Getaway Retreat......................................239

25 The Senior Resource Center Extravaganza............245

26 Santo Domingo Connection..............................253

27 New Mexico Bound...259

28 At Last, A Place of Our Own.............................273

29 Some Extraordinary Events..............................277

Introduction

From an early age my sister and I were already riding on the coat 'tales', literally, of our mother. She took us along on many magical adventures. Sometimes we thought we went to the far edges of the earth, and beyond. We went happily and were most often delighted by the different sights, sounds and smells of new and foreign surroundings. Sometimes though we felt like we were hanging on for dear life. And what a life it has been.

Our mom entertained and enchanted us with her stories, skits and dances. Running around the living room draped in scarves, curtains and feather boas. Twirling and dancing to the sounds of Swan Lake, The Tijuana Brass and The Girl From Ipanema. Harry Belafonte's "Day light comes..." is still one of my favorites.

Early memories of our own magical journey include being baptized as Lutherans, marching for peace with the Unitarians, hosting Native American elders who prepared acorn mush for us, (yuck), and learning to sing Hava Nagila and dance the Horah. Some of our mom's many talents were teaching arts and crafts to kids our ages at various camps and classes.

Our mom demonstrated to us, as young girls, and now as grown women, that we could choose to participate in endless selfless causes and spontaneous adventures. We learned early on how to pick up and go forward, unafraid, to explore new places and enjoy different experiences.

We've lived by the Pacific Ocean where we collected, cooked and ate seaweed and mussels. Hiked in the Redwoods, the Sierras, the Grand Canyon, the Blue Hole and the Sangre de Cristo Mountains; plus many more majestic places.

Our journey was like the song, "this land is your land, this land is my land...". We were definitely on, "the ribbon of highway".

Our own individual paths have been quite a trip and just a small part of our mom's magical journey. The following stories are all true. We are both privileged indeed to be a part of this story. We hope you enjoy.

Julie and Cyndi

Preface

My book title, Me and My Magical Life, highlights the magic elements in my life. The use of Me and My in the title addresses the nuisance level bi-polar disorder that has been like a rudder in my life, sometimes steering me into uncharted territory. I have often felt that my life has the bi-polar disorder and I get swept along as an observer. Buying a one-way ticket at age 35 to Mexico was an out of body experience that I still marvel at after all these years. And that was just one event.

As a young woman during the sixties and seventies I spent a lot of time working on raising my conscious awareness, much to the chagrin of my spouse and family. I married young, in 1955 when a wife "belonged" to her husband. That never felt right to me. This book is about how that played out over time. The level of awareness I achieved made it possible. In my eighty-third year, I can tell you that I learned to get out of my own way and trust my conscious and subconscious decisions to lead me in the right direction. I had plenty of detractors along the way, but I never gave in to ridicule or criticism; some powerful drive had taken over and swept me forward toward a life full of possibilities. There is fulfillment and richness in my life that could not have been possible without the stories in this book. I feel like a successful artist, a successful writer, wife, and mother. And best of all, I feel like a successful woman for taking all those risks. And the magical events continue.

Not long after I published Accidental Anthropologists, I discovered a box of stories I had written years earlier. Accidental Anthropologists was published five years ago using a pseudonym, Claudia Clavel, to protect the identity of my neighbors. For that reason, all the names were changed. This book doesn't present that problem, but it created another: whether to reveal the real name of the author of Accidental Anthropologists.

But back to my box of stories: I was surprised to see how far back some of the stories had taken place, and I was even more surprised to find how much material had been accumulated. Rather than keeping a journal, I wrote stories about events that were taking place in my life. The one theme that kept coming up was the magic in my life and how that related to colorful people and extraordinary events that kept coming. Once I recognized a way out of darkness, I let go of fear and held on for dear life.

I want to thank all the people who have encouraged and supported my writing throughout the years. I have been telling stories since I can remember. Without the support of those around me, my stories would not have made it into book form. My old friend, Ramona Gault has done a fine job as copy editor and adviser. My amazing husband did the graphic design book layout and cover, and he has been there for me every step of the way. I have a wonderful group of women friends who continue to add expertise and color to my creative life. Beverly and Hal Jackson have to be mentioned, for without their encouragement, Accidental Anthropologists would not have been published. As we know, one thing tends to lead to another: Me, and My Magic Life came out of that beginning.

I couldn't stop thinking about why I wanted to tell my story, and then it dawned on me: The purpose of this book is to remind readers that our ancestors play a huge part in our future lives. Both of my grandmothers were born in the 1800's. The two women divorced at a time when it was unthinkable. My maternal grandmother went on to be married 5 times. Eva and Idella were among the original feminists of their time. I have to believe that I have genes from both women, but their stories are even more important to me. Intuitively, I felt that I didn't have to stay in a bad situation.

Over time, hearing my grandmother's stories subconsciously sunk in and gave methe courage to change my life.

I have never known anything about family members beyond my grandparents and I was determined to alter that fact. I want my grandchildren and beyond to know what they are capable of in their own lives because of those who have come before them. That's why inspirational stories are so important; either as oral histories, or written stories.

1
Vision

I have had a lot of dreams during my life, but only a few had staying power. Dreams are usually fleeting, but one of those was so powerful and lasting it eventually transformed my life. The dream did not seem so profound at the time because I was married, but it would later prove to be prophetic. It had to do with a man named David or Michael, and he was either a writer or a photographer. The dream woke me from a deep sleep while I was married to a man who had been my husband for eighteen years and within a year or two, would become my ex-husband.

The image of David or Michael, writer or photographer, was so powerful it burned an image into my consciousness that was to last forever. It was not so much the names or vocations that shook me, but an incredible feeling of peace and comfort that I had never known before. That and the feeling that eventually everything within my chaotic world would be right with the universe. It was not something I dwelt on, just that I accepted it as fact and fate. I did not go out looking for this person.

My life has never been quite usual, in the sense that interesting and colorful people have somehow always found their way to my doorstep. Even in suburbia, or the middle of nowhere. Even when I was married to Fabian Klooster, my first husband, a conservative Minnesota farm boy. I tried very hard to live a "regular" life in suburban Sacramento, California, striving to fit into the status quo. I played bridge for years with a group of seven wonderful women who were participating moms in one of the first cooperative preschools in the country during the early sixties. I was a very creative housewife who took evening art classes and read piles of books and had lots of fun in the process. Julie and Cyndi claim to this day that they had wonderful and ideal childhoods. I know that is a stretch, but it is comforting to think they feel that way, especially in view of the way things turned out for us all.

During that time a lot of stuff was going on that was shaking me to the core. It had finally dawned on me that my husband not only was being unfaithful, but also had a severe gambling addiction that was turning him into a habitual liar. I had found paper proof of the discrepancies, so I could no longer turn my head away from the facts. Unfortunately, none of what he was doing was new, for five years earlier I had actually caught him with the goods, so to speak. He had come home with lipstick smeared all over his shirt, and something made me go directly to the credit union, where my worst fears were realized. He had spent all the money in our savings and a woman had forged my name on a bank loan. I was ready to leave him then, but first I wanted to talk to my parents because I had great respect for them, and their long marriage. They had never interfered in my adult life so I felt them to be a safe haven in light of the shattering experience I was dealing with. After telling my story, there was a long pause and finally my father spoke. He said, "You are probably such a bitch to live with, the guy is justified in his actions." My mother took it from there as

Me and My Magical Life

she added, "You go home and try to be a better wife." I could hardly believe my ears. It was the most completely crushing blow I had ever experienced. I remember my ears ringing so loudly I could no longer hear anything. I rushed out of their house and prayed to die on the spot.

That was nineteen sixty-five, and I saw myself as the world saw me: a housewife/sometime artist. How could I possibly strike out on my own and survive? Our family doctor was also our good friend with whom we spent a lot of time, so I phoned him when I arrived home. Howard came right over after hearing my story and gave me a shot to calm me down, and then tried to talk "sense" to me. He asked how I could leave with two young children? What would I do without health insurance, life insurance? How would I support myself? That pretty much did it for me. I was damned to a life of misery.

It took the next five years for me to reach another place, and it came about because of Murray Lundberg, a fifteen-year-old boy who looked at me through the lens of his four-by-five camera when I was picking strawberries. I had said on introduction that I was "only" a housewife/artist, and without knowing my story, out of the blue, the boy said he did not see the woman who I thought I was at the time. He said he saw a completely different person. For the first time in my life I had a glimpse of who that might be, and it was to change my life forever. It was not long after that when I experienced the dream of David or Michael, writer or photographer.

While still married, and living in a rural setting, one day, a white boy showed up at our door along with nine Blackfeet Indian kids. His name was Murray and he was to have a profound effect on all our lives. Murray and the others were brought to us by their teacher, Barry

McWilliams, his wife, Cathy, and their one-year-old son, Colin. They came from Browning, Montana, on their way to Southern California for a visit to Disneyland. They arrived at our house for food and shelter and to pick up my daughter Julie, who had been a student of Barry's two years before when we had all lived in Half Moon Bay, California. Barry was a charismatic English teacher of middle school and high school students, but he usually never stayed in one place for more than a year or two. At Half Moon Bay, the teacher took his English classes to the beach on foggy days, where they sat listening to the pounding surf and pondering for a while before returning to the classroom to write haiku. We still have a book of that student poetry and it is quite wonderful. That man could inspire!

Barry's departures were always abrupt, given his nature for adventure, and always emotional for the students he left behind. When he drove off in the fog from Half Moon Bay middle school with a sofa tied on top of his truck, two dogs barking wildly in the back, and kids running down the street after him crying their eyes out, you knew this was a teacher they would never forget. As a former teacher friend from that school reminded me more than thirty years later, she and the other teachers cried for their loss and have never forgotten Barry either.

So the white boy, nine Blackfeet teenagers, and the McWilliams family spent two nights with us, resting before the next leg of their trip. From our place, the group had another four hundred miles to their destination. They planned to camp in the back yard of the home of Barry's childhood friend's parents, who lived near Disneyland. Little did any of us know that one day in the not too distant future, these same people would become my new in-laws. My daughter Julie actually met my

Me and My Magical Life

future husband at his parents' home while camping in their back yard. The two of them met nearly two years before he and I would meet, in another far-away place, under even stranger circumstances. Neither of them remembered the event until we were all living together, in a place far from Disneyland.

During the group's rest, my family learned more than we wanted to know about life on an Indian reservation, as told from the mouths of teenagers. Every one of them had scars from knife fights they had encountered at riverbank drinking parties with their rival Blood Indian (Kainai Nation) neighbors across the river in Canada. It seemed to me the girls had more scars than the boys, and as both groups pointed out, girls fought differently than boys so their wounds were in different places. My daughters were eleven and fourteen at the time, and their eyes grew round as they listened to the stories of our guests. I remember feeling sick to my stomach at the thought of those children living such brutal lives. Especially when they had absolutely nothing to look forward to in their future. It was a very sobering experience for us as a family.

The lone white boy of the group was another story altogether. Murray Lundberg was fifteen years old. He was the son of the building contractor who was constructing new houses on the Blackfeet reservation. The boy was one of the most precocious kids we had ever encountered; it was something you knew the minute you looked into his eyes. I admit that I stared at the boy for an instant too long, and it was because his eyes had the oddest appearance; there was a bluish film covering both of Murray's eyes. I wondered about that as I finally turned my gaze away from his face.

Charlotte Plantz

The minute Murray opened his mouth and began to speak there was no doubt that he was a very different teenage boy. For one thing, he was completely comfortable in the presence of adults. I noticed a slightly devilish smile as he was speaking, as though he were completely aware of the impression he was having on you while the words were tumbling out of his mouth, sophisticated words that were far and above most kids his age.

The other amazing thing about Murray was the fact that he was just as comfortable with his Indian peers. In no way did he speak down to them. In fact, you could feel the mutual respect they had for one another as they bantered among themselves. I remember smiling as I surveyed the mismatched group that would be fed and housed by my family for those few days, and thinking that just knowing Barry McWilliams ensured adventure at every turn.

After dinner, we sat up until the wee hours of the morning, talking and telling stories. I was sure those kids slept the entire four hundred miles to Disneyland. Julie did go on the trip and had a wonderful time, and as I recall, the group returned by the same route in order to drop off our daughter. We must have done the whole routine over again, and it's odd that I remember the arrival in vivid detail and not the departure. We must all have been exhausted by that time.

Actually, over the past fifty years that we have known Barry, every visit usually ended with plaster falling off the walls, a door coming apart in someone's hands, a water pipe breaking and shooting water straight up out of the toilet, or horses getting loose and rampaging through the neighborhood. Something dramatic enough that we looked at one another and knew the visit was over-really over, with Barry rushing to his truck before anything else could possibly go awry. Things usually began to physically fall apart after three days, so you had to plan accordingly. It also meant that a lot of activity, verbal or physical, took place in a short period of time, so that it was always an intense experience. Intense. Wonderful. And always-exciting.

2
MURRAY

One afternoon several months after the McWilliams group had come and gone, the telephone rang and I was surprised to hear the caller identify himself as Murray Lundberg. He asked whether I remembered him from the Montana group? I assured him that I did. The boy said he had moved to San Francisco with his father's reluctant blessing and had a job at Brooks Camera as a salesman. Perhaps he could sense my amazement at the absurdity of the statement, for he added that he had recently turned sixteen, as if that would change my response. Murray continued, telling me that he was living as a caretaker at an alternative school. He said it worked out perfectly since he worked all day, and by the time he returned in the evening the students had gone home.

Hearing that, I burst out laughing. What Murray was telling me was so far from the world in which I lived. So far from anything I could imagine. Julie had recently turned fifteen, and I kept trying to see her in a similar circumstance but my mind could not conjure up an image of any kind. Just listening to Murray with an open mind made me feel a bit like I was contributing to his truancy. I remember saying as much to him, but he only laughed, saying he finally felt that he was doing the right thing with his life. At sixteen he was that sure of himself.

But then, he had convinced the largest camera store in the state to hire him, and it was not long before he was made a manager!

Murray moved through life at the speed of a comet and was so comfortable with adults that within a short time he had integrated himself into a group of elderly women who gathered weekly to discuss books they were reading. I was a voracious reader, but Murray's reading list put me to shame. He had already read more classics than I knew existed and was forever calling me up to tell me I simply had to read Thomas Hardy, Herman Hesse, or perhaps James Joyce. He once jumped off a bus in Miami while visiting his family to race to a phone booth and call me to demand that I read Jude the Obscure. One of the characters in the book was named Charlotte, and she reminded him of me. It was by then apparent to me that Murray had developed a teenage crush on me. By the time I finished reading Jude the Obscure I was certain of that. I talked to my husband and daughters about Murray's infatuation with me, and we all agreed that even though he was a pretty weird kid, he would probably grow out of it and settle down and become a "normal" guy.

Given Murray's background, there was little chance that he would ever live a "normal" life. He had been born into a wealthy Florida family, late in his parents' marriage. The couple had two daughters, one of whom was eighteen years old when Murray was born. The other sister was slightly younger, but they were pretty much out of the house by the time Murray was born. His father was an accomplished violinist, who by the time I met his son was playing with the Tucson Symphony during the six months the family resided in Arizona. The remainder of their year was spent on Biscayne Island in Florida, where Murray's mother, Molly, worked as a real estate agent for other wealthy clients. Her husband, Les, ran the Murray Corp., a family contracting business that specialized in government contracts around the country.

I remember once when Murray received a letter from his mother written on Murray Corp. memo notes, his face became red and distorted as he crumpled the papers up and hurled them on the floor. He remarked that for her part, all their communication was on a business level. It infuriated him to the end of his life. His father was the complete opposite, a wonderfully warm, loving man who knew his son's inner turmoil and tried to help him in whatever ways he could. Les wanted Murray to realize all of his dreams because he had spent nearly all his life doing everything he could to provide a good life for his family while denying his own talent as a violinist. The violin was the man's true passion, and fortunately he was able, toward the end of his life, to realize some of that dream when playing with the symphony.

That was the sole reason Les agreed to allow his son to set up a life for himself alone, at the age of sixteen, in San Francisco, without any interference from his family. Murray remained financially independent from his parents except in extreme instances, and I am sure that impressed his father as well. It certainly impressed all of us who knew him. In fact, that is probably the one reason my husband at the time allowed Murray to become such a part of our lives. That, and Murray could charm a snake. It was a survival technique learned early on in his life, and he would use it to the end.

Murray was of the counterculture era, circa nineteen seventy, San Francisco. He was tall, close to six feet two inches. He was thin, with a shock of jet-black hair that grew not quite to his shoulders. He had a small mouth with thin lips, and his nose was small as well, and it turned up at the end. Jet-black eyebrows drew your attention to his strange eyes, which not only were piercing; they had that glazed look I mentioned before. We eventually learned that at age ten, Murray and a friend were experimenting with household cleaners, and they mixed a can of Draino with bleach. It exploded in Murray's face, instantly blinding him. Had it not been for a quick-thinking maid and a swimming pool, he would have been left permanently blinded. The glaze covering his eyeballs was scar tissue, and it did give him the appearance of being slightly otherworldly. As time passed, that seemed more and more likely to all who knew him.

Murray's choice of clothing was perfectly appropriate for that era. Like so many kids in rebellion, and especially those born into wealth, clothing gave him the opportunity to express a completely different persona. For him, that was easy to attain in the thrift stores of San Francisco. He always wore sandals without socks, even in winter, and his shirts were at least a size too large, so they hung limp and shapeless on his thin body.

By today's standards, Murray was an exact replica of a street person, but at that time he was one happy fellow, living the perfect life. I don't believe I ever saw him without a camera slung over one shoulder. He was a gifted photographer, especially at that early age, and that was in part due to the charm I mentioned earlier. He could capture the most incredible photographs of people, just by asking them to pose for him.

Shortly after his arrival in the City, Murray approached a well-known photographer to ask whether he could study with her. Her name was Imogen Cunningham, and she was a contemporary of Ansel Adams and Minor White during the heyday of black-and-white photography. Ms. Cunningham was in her nineties when Murray approached her, and she agreed to allow him to join a small group of students. Sadly, very soon their personalities clashed, and she asked him to leave her studio, never to return. Rather than being devastated, Murray was amused by the incident and never ceased to admire her work as an artist.

I saw a documentary on Imogen Cunningham's life a number of years later. The film opened with her standing next to a trash can in the middle of the San Francisco National Cemetery. The old woman was rolling ribbon she had fished out of the can, grousing about the terrible waste going on in the country. Cunningham had a wry sense of humor and told a wonderful story about Ansel Adams and a Folgers Coffee can with a panorama of Yosemite Valley reproduced from one of his photographs. As she told it, a group of Adams's peers had been giving him a bad time of it for "going commercial," and she wanted to get her licks in.

The old woman filled one of the cans with a plant and hired a boy to carry it to Adams. She said, "The plant was something he could smoke if he wanted"! No wonder Murray was amused. Amazingly, years before I saw the documentary, an Ansel Adams coffee can came into my life, and I treasure it to this day. We use it to store rolled oats.

So Murray, like our friend Barry, was an adventure unto himself. Not only was he precocious, but over time we would learn he was prescient as well. Murray wove in and out of our life, as a family, for the next year and a half, usually showing up unannounced in his sandals and baggy shirts. It got to be a joke in the family that when any of us had a thought about what Murray might be up to, the phone rang or he turned up at our door. His backpack was always filled with books and camera equipment, and he had a hundred stories to tell. Murray never ceased to educate, amaze, and entertain us, and we lingered around the dinner table for hours whenever he showed up.

One freezing, foggy winter night, Murray called from a pay phone a few miles away. He said it was too late to hitch a ride so could somebody pick him up. He added that he was not alone; he had a traveling companion. My husband set off to pick them up, grumbling slightly at the thought of a stranger in our midst.

When they arrived back at the house, Murray introduced us to his friend, a young man who looked positively done in. It took a moment for me to realize Murray's friend was not wearing a jacket. I thought perhaps he was one of those warm-blooded types. But then I noticed he was shivering slightly so I asked if he would like to take a hot shower to warm up. I have never seen anyone so relieved by such a simple offer. By the time he had warmed his body and filled his stomach with quickly prepared leftovers, the young man looked in much better shape. After a glass of wine his spirit brightened as well.

After my husband had gone to bed, and I had the young man settled in the spare room, Julie, Murray, and I lingered at the table, catching up on his life in the great city by the bay. Not until saying goodnight did he tell me that the young man was AWOL from an army psychiatric hospital. He was trying to hitchhike to his home in Nebraska. The two young men had met on the roadside, hitching out of the city, and they decided to travel together. Murray told me he simply could not leave the guy out in the freezing fog. He knew we would be sympathetic. He also told me the young man was an artist and realized the military was the wrong place for him. That was probably why he wound up in a psychiatric unit.

The next morning after breakfast, I found an old jacket of my husband's, packed a sandwich, apple, and some cookies, and then remembered a small, spare drawing pad. I added some pencils to a cloth bag and then drove the young man to the interstate highway, where he would continue his journey. When we stopped, I handed him the lunch bag and art supplies, saying perhaps he could amuse himself while waiting for rides. His eyes welled up with tears as he leaned across the seat and kissed me on the cheek.

After Murray had gone back to the city, my husband declared that we should not be so open about taking strangers into our home. He added that the young man could have been a murderer or something. I assured him that Murray would never bring a murderer into our home. However, I did not mention the AWOL aspect; instead I told him how grateful the young man had been for our hospitality.

Our family drove to San Francisco one Saturday morning to visit Murray at the alternative school where he was living. He had invited us to spend the weekend so he could show us around his world and prepare dinner for us. It was probably that visit that pointed out to me the vast differences between suburbia and the multicultural world of a great city.

Folsom, California, in the late fifties and early sixties was a magnet for people from all over the country seeking a new life in the aerospace industry. Pay was good and opportunity for advancement was promising.

It was an exciting time and place for young married couples to settle into a comfortable life among a group of like-minded peers. My husband worked as a machinist where everyone felt like a pioneer, charting new territory in the high-tech world of jet engines and rocket boosters.

For the first few years, we lived in a neighborhood of blue-collar machinists and technicians. Because I had become involved in a new cooperative preschool, our friends and acquaintances consisted of white-collar families. They were engineers, bankers, teachers, and doctors; notable only because it was my first brush with the caste system of America. It was not long before our blue-collar neighbors let me know that we were stepping out of our league.

Neighbors were not the only finger-pointers. My parents both worked at Aerojet as technicians, and several of our new friends were not only neighbors of my parents, but their superiors in the workplace as well. It did not help when my husband and I became part of a bridge group consisting of seven other couples that would go on for many years. My parents could not bear the thought that I was a part of that group, something I never understood. Those same people probably saved my sanity because they were (and are) quite simply wonderful human beings.

We not only played bridge together but also spent weekends in the mountains camping, or in cabins at the seashore with all our children. There were always crafts projects and nature hikes, snow trips, and progressive Thanksgiving dinners. We had theme parties for the children at lake and river beaches or at the Aerojet family center swimming pool. In most aspects it was an ideal life for our little family, and my daughters recall that period as among the happiest in their lives.

Me and My Magical Life

Sadly, I was tormented by my inability to "stay in my own place." My thirst for knowledge and culture continued to drive me to the edge of acceptance by my own family and neighbors. But nothing could stop me, not even myself. As I stood in the hall of that San Francisco alternative school, I knew my life was already in the throes of change, and nothing was going to alter the direction it was headed. My husband knew it too. I knew he hated being at that school. It represented another part of life that was repugnant to him: a world of mixed races, young people, wild ideas, and books and music. The school represented all the things that threatened his world and made his wife a mystery to him. From that day forward, my husband threw himself into his secret world of honky-tonk bars and beehive hairdo women-and especially into gambling.

We had already grown apart mentally, spiritually, and emotionally. The physical act would take a bit longer. It took a while before my mind could comprehend what had happened, but eventually I stepped out into the glare of sunlight and a hopeful future. Our young friend Murray, who knew nothing of what had taken place in my life, had looked at me through his camera lens and seen a different woman. On reflection, that was all it took. I knew I would soon be a free woman.

In 1966, we moved to Half Moon Bay, California, where we lived nearly four years. It proved to be one of the most creative periods of my life, and I established myself as a professional artist. Before that, however, I worked part-time in the office of the San Mateo County Farm Advisors, where I sat in a little back room typing endless lists of labels for events. One day, the office staff roared with laughter when I emerged from my den to declare that I could only type fast if I was wearing sneakers laced tightly. That kind of reaction made me think about how I was spending my time.

Within a couple of years I knew that my time should be spent making art. I can't remember a time when art was not a central part of my life. I had to quit my job, even though I loved the people and enjoyed the mindless act of typing lists. Pat Dutra was the office manager and we had a wonderful dark-humored relationship, so it was fitting that my going-away cake had black icing with a skull and crossbones for decoration. The word "Traitor" had been written as large as possible. Pat later became the first person to collect my art, and she remained a supporter of my talent for many years. The minute I quit my job, I threw myself into creating as full time as possible with two young daughters and a traditional meat-and-potatoes husband. To his credit, Fabian was always good about helping with household chores and giving me creative space.

Our time in Half Moon Bay was creatively perfect for me. I had previously established myself in Sacramento as a batik artist, so I didn't hesitate when a group of artists asked if I would be interested in joining a cooperative art gallery that was in the process of being formed. Eventually the group constructed a steel building that became the center of a compound of smaller shops operated by craftspeople. The gallery came together quickly, so there was little time to think. To become a part of it required a body of work, and that became my priority. By the time the gallery held the opening reception, we had moved back to Folsom. I traveled back and forth for the next year, producing a steady flow of batiks to replace those that sold sometimes as quickly as they were hung on the gallery wall.

Me and My Magical Life

I was amazed and encouraged by the acceptance and support I received from the gallery artists, and delighted by the number of sales. The group nudged me into professionalism at a time when I was feeling insecure about calling myself a real artist. A number of gallery artists were well established in San Francisco and the surrounding Bay Area, and they lifted me up with them. I joined the San Francisco Artists Guild and showed in many outdoor art shows, establishing myself even further as a reputable artist. And then I stopped creating. I simply ran dry and realized the art was no longer coming from the right place, but I had enough work for the Half Moon Bay Gallery to keep sales going for the next year. It was a one hundred mile drive between cities and I made the trip fairly often for shows.

Going back to Folsom wasn't difficult. I began teaching batik classes in an adult education program two evenings a week, and I drove way out in the country to teach art at a Boys Ranch for incarcerated teens one night a week, so I kept busy and creative. Eventually I was able to produce more art to sell, but I never fully recovered my previous successful run. Looking back, I am amazed to see the pattern of my creative existence; no matter how bad things ever got in my life, art was the driving force that kept me sane and on track. For some weird reason, it also helped me stay married. I still felt that I could not survive without the support of a man. In my mind I was a wife and mother first. Art was something I did on the side, even though I had become successful at it.

3
A Plan From Out of the Blue

But then came a plan from out of the blue. In the spring of 1972, we began receiving letters from Barry McWilliams, regaling us with the beauty and charms of Northern New Mexico, where he and his little family had recently settled. He described the tiny village of Chacon and its inhabitants, who were ancestors of the Spanish conquistadores who had explored the region during the mid-fifteen hundreds. Barry said their Spanish was so archaic it was not understood to Mexicans south of the border.

The letter writer described, in detail, little mud houses with steep tin roofs and men who plowed fields with teams of horses. Because it was spring, the adventurer also painted a picture of fields of wild irises, followed by clumps of wild, tiny pink rose bushes. The village was in a setting of steep mountains that rose to over 10,000 feet on both sides of the narrow valley. The fields had been divided into narrow strips running from mountaintop to the river below, portioned out among sons as they reached manhood.

I couldn't remember ever being so taken by someone's descriptions of a place. It sounded like the most exotic, romantic adventure in the world. The fact that I knew someone who lived in that place shook me out of my stupor. It didn't take long before I knew that was where I had to go in order to learn survival skills for my future life.

Fabian's family lived in a very small town in southwestern Minnesota, a place his parents had retired to after farming all their lives. We had visited there only a couple of times when our girls were young. It was apparent from the beginning that I was very different from Minnesotans. His family was nice to me, but we knew that it was probably better that we stayed in California and wrote occasional letters. In my plan from out of the blue, I decided it was time for another visit so the girls could see their grandparents before they grew much older. It was also a reason for visiting New Mexico. I had saved some money and was determined to have a summer experience with my daughters in that remote and exotic place.

I had never been very far from home before, except for an overnight with friends when transporting art to the Bay Area, so I was surprised by my determination to follow through with the trip. I invited my husband to join us as far as New Mexico because I knew he would have to get back to his machine shop. I arranged for him to fly out of Albuquerque after a few days' visit with the McWilliams family. Something powerful had risen up in me, and there was no argument regarding the plan. I had recently purchased a 1965 Mercedes for $1,500, and it was in excellent shape for driving across country. For the first time in years I felt the possibility of my own survival within grasp.

If there had been any doubt in my mind about where I fit into the universe, visiting Minnesota again convinced me that I was now on the right track. The talk between Fabian's brother and cousins turned to retirement and fishing trips, and trailers parked next to lakes for weeks on end. It was a wake-up call, and I realized that I had not been paying attention to the reality of my own future life with the man I had married. When we arrived in Chacon, New Mexico, the reality became more than apparent: Fabian was horrified and more than terrified by what he encountered.

Barry had not exaggerated. In fact, it was even more unique than he had described. The people of the valley had always been poor; trying to eke out a living at that altitude, with one of the shortest growing seasons in the country, was more than daunting. Added to that, the weather could change on a dime on any given day. The mud houses seemed ancient; some were tilting precariously while smoke still puffed up out of crooked stovepipes. It was hard to imagine that people lived within those mud walls. Compared to the neatly organized farm communities we had just traveled through in Minnesota and Iowa, the Chacon valley appeared to us as a foreign country on a different continent.

Many houses, fallen into ruin, were sprinkled along the little highway that followed the river to the end of the valley, where two mountain ranges came together. The road stopped at the end of the valley, and you had to turn around and go back the way you came in. We followed Barry's map that left the paved road and meandered down through hay fields to the river, where the crossing was over old wood planks that shuddered as you drove to the other side. As we climbed up from the river we saw several houses sitting on the side of the mountain and were relieved that we had found our way.

We stopped at the first house, where an old Studebaker was parked in front. Before I could get out of the car, an older man came out to greet us. He said he was Ben Cordova. Tiny, thin, and wiry, Mr. Cordova was a retired judge from the little city of Las Vegas, 45 miles down the mountains. He and his wife planned to live out their remaining years in that remote spot, driving the old Studebaker in and out through mud and snow that hampered most people. Many a time that summer when we were stuck in deep, slick, clay mud, Mr. Cordova would drive by slowly, with a smile and wave of his hand. He was much too old to help anybody out of the muck, and I was certain he must have taken some pleasure in his unique driving skills.

Barry's neighbor informed us we were nearly at our destination and pointed to the small adobe houses behind his place, indicating that was where Barry, Cathy, and Colin lived. He also told us they were not at home, but had gone into Las Vegas for supplies. We were to make ourselves comfortable until their return. The house was unlocked and Barry had erected a large tent where we would be sleeping. Julie and Cyndi were wide-eyed, while my husband's eyes narrowed to slits as he took in the sorry state of the place, including the outhouse, which actually seemed in pretty good shape to me. A wringer washer sat on the front porch, and piles of junk and rubble were strewn all over the ground.

Even though it was June, the air was cool at that altitude, and beautiful white clouds formed over the highest peaks. The view out over the long valley took my breath away. I felt I had died and gone to heaven. Our family had nothing to do but sit back and relax until the McWilliams clan returned. It wasn't long before we heard them coming, before we saw the truck climbing up from the crude bridge. The dogs had already jumped out and were running alongside the truck. By the time they reached the yard and realized strangers were in their midst, the dogs were wild with excitement. We walked out to meet the family and were surprised to see two other bodies climbing out of the pickup bed. One was Murray, grinning from ear to ear. He hadn't told us he would be there; we thought he had gone to Florida to see his parents. What a wonderful surprise.

The other body was that of a man of medium height and build with a pleasant face and a full beard. He was smiling as we approached, and Barry introduced us to his childhood friend, Mike Plantz. His actual name was David Michael Plantz, and he was in that gorgeous place working on a photography project with Murray and a couple of other Anglos who lived in another remote area. I could sense displeasure from my husband due to the presence of the two men who would become a part of our summer adventure. I, on the other hand, was delighted because it all had to do with creativity. After Mike and I became a couple, he told me that Murray said to him on their way back from Las Vegas that day we arrived, "You are going to love meeting Charlotte." I did not make the connection to my dream from two years before, and would not for a long time. A great many life-changing events would take place before that happened.

Cathy and I prepared a meal and we spent the evening wandering around the place, marveling at the wealth of ancient tools and equipment scattered around a shed. The second mud house, which was being used as a darkroom by Murray and Mike, was about fifteen feet away from Barry and Cathy's home. Over time, they had learned from experience that the little adobe was haunted. That was verified by the owner, Pedro, who had told them from the time he could remember, the house had always had a ghost. We laughed when the photographers showed us the old wringer washing machine out in the yard where they washed their prints. It was a primitive operation to say the least, but quite productive given the number of prints strewn all over a table in the darkroom.

Murray and Mike had been riding horseback into some remote areas around the valley, using Murray's charm to persuade local folks to allow their pictures to be taken. Few people there owned cameras, so locals were open to the idea of having their pictures taken. The photographers made sure the subjects received copies of their photos, which was the barter system the two used all over the valley and into other areas as their reputations grew.

Mike described a couple they had photographed who lived in an isolated, two-room adobe with doorways so small Mike and Murray had to bend down to enter. Once they were indoors, their heads brushed the ceiling. The elderly couple herded goats and sheep. They were tiny and as agile as their herds. The photographs were beautiful and historical as well, because by then the outside world was closing in. As it turned out, Murray and Mike were among the few Anglo outsiders who were allowed to live in the valley, and only then because of Pedro and Bessie Abeyta, who were about to become my landlords as well as the McWilliams's.

Our family spent the night in the tent that had been set up in a grove of wild plum and apple trees. I thrilled at the sound of wind blowing through the trees, lulling me to sleep. The next day, Barry took us to meet the Abeyta family and to look at the house they had agreed to rent to us for the summer. Pedro and Bessie lived down on the paved road nearly across from the post office that was, in reality, a small trailer. The Abeytas had six children: three boys and three girls, two of whom were the same ages as Julie, who was sixteen and Cyndi, thirteen. Their boys had a rock and roll band and practiced often, so there was always something for the Chacon kids to do.

The band members drove a van that held all of their equipment and they played at events around the Mora Valley. My daughters and the Abeyta girls were invited to accompany the boy band to various functions throughout the summer. Pedro and Bessie, along with their family, were to become close, lifelong friends. They were uncommonly open and aware in that remote place, mainly due to their children, who opened up their world beyond the Sangre de Cristo Mountains. The family helped many a Vista worker sort out details of life in that little-known world, and they hosted foreign exchange students and friends made in other places beyond the confines of their secluded valley.

The rock and roll van transported children to cultural events in Las Vegas and on to Santa Fe for the Opera in summer. All six Abeyta children would go on to college and exemplary careers in various fields. All but one remained in New Mexico, where they married and raised families within a fifty-mile radius of their birthplace.

The bonds are that strong. I immediately found that more than appealing because I came from a culture where, by the time I was an adult, extended families had disappeared. Our grandparents, aunts, uncles, and cousins were distant, elusive entities who had faded away into oblivion. The Hispanic culture also made me aware of how precious a family unit was and reminded me why I had stayed married for so many years to the wrong man.

We followed Pedro and Bessie in their pickup truck along a dirt track about a quarter of a mile behind their house to the little adobe that would become our home for the summer. The house sat next to an arroyo on the side of a mountain with the Mora River running about 150 feet below. There were no trees, but a lot of wild rose bushes grew around the house. Everything else had been eaten down to the ground by cows that roamed the mountainsides. Pedro owned around 500 acres, so there were a lot of cows grazing and reproducing.

There were no cows when we arrived, but plenty of other livestock milling around. There were ducks, geese, chickens, guinea hens, and a horse. The horse fell in love with me immediately and followed me everywhere. That included the outhouse, which had no door. And it wasn't just the horse; the poultry flock followed me as well. During those visits I had to employ a lot of shouting and shooing in order to find relief. It was the same whenever I entered the back door to the house; the horse walked up to the door and if I didn't push him away, he would walk right inside the house. Pedro laughed about that all summer. He also told us to beware of the largest goose. He said the gander was mean and liked to pinch.

As I stood surveying the old adobe house that leaned a bit and the menagerie gathered around us, I began having doubts about my sanity. I had chosen to spend nearly three months in a house with no running water, and an outhouse with no door that was built in the shape of a tepee so the wind wouldn't blow it over. And then I thought about sitting in the privy admiring the view and having to kick my feet to keep the animals from coming in to join me.

My husband was speechless, and I still can't believe my teenage daughters agreed to stay there with me. The three-room house was wired for electricity and contained a wood cookstove as well as a small wood heater in the back room. The roof was steeply pitched to keep the snow from piling up in winter. The whole structure tilted forward, so that if you spilled something in one spot it would run downhill to another room.

There was a bed platform, but no mattress, although there was a couch that could accommodate Cyndi. Julie and I would have to figure out something for our needs soon. The house did contain a refrigerator, kitchen table, and chairs for four. A large overstuffed chair next to the woodstove looked appealing. A cupboard for dishes and staple food items took up one wall. There were also mice. There were droppings in every room.

I was terrified of mice and other wild creatures, and why I didn't run for home is still a mystery to me. It appeared I was so determined to learn survival skills that I would face anything at that point. We would have to bathe in the river between afternoon thunderstorms, carry water from the Abeytas' house, and chop our own firewood. The concept became both terrifying and exhilarating. My husband laughed scornfully when he surveyed the pile of rotten lumber and the rusted axe behind the house. I knew it was time to get him out of there, or he would undermine all my self-confidence and destroy my chances of surviving on my own. It had become my odyssey and nothing would stand in my way.

The next day, Julie, Cyndi, Murray, and I drove Fabian the 175 miles to the Albuquerque airport. We hugged and kissed our father/husband goodbye and watched his plane take off. In that instant, I knew I was already divorced. The entire trip to Minnesota and New Mexico had been the final stages of separation. The feeling was of such great relief that I burst into tears on the spot. From that moment on, I felt so empowered that life became a series of magical events that provided us with everything we needed to survive.

Charlotte Plantz

Fabian's departure had been planned carefully to coincide with the arrival of Julie's friend Sean. It was not long before her plane arrived from Sacramento, and we able to greet her with open arms. It did occur to me that I was a mother who was about to lead her children into a foreign place, full of dangerous potentials. It would be the greatest adventure any of us had ever undertaken. It was important that we all learn as much as possible from the experience so we could become stronger, more secure human beings. My exuberance and positive attitude would see us through. At least, that's what I thought.

4
Chacon Summer

My great enthusiasm for the summer adventure became infectious, especially with the addition of Sean to our group. She and Julie had been school chums since ninth grade, and she was a fountain of creative energy. Sean was the perfect addition to our expedition. We drove back up the mountain fully ready to solve all the problems presented to us. I had brought a unique English shower apparatus, and for the girls, that was a priority since they weren't so keen to bathe in the river.

A plastic curtain was suspended from a ring that was hung over a spike. The spike was nailed into one of the log vigas that supported the roof. The five-gallon black water bag that had been warming in the sun was transferred to a pump container. The bather stood in a square plastic tub and pumped hot water into a shower hose that had a nozzle resembling a telephone receiver. You had to lather up and rinse off quickly so as not to waste water. The shower worked for me on rainy days, but otherwise I preferred bathing in the river in the afternoons between thunderstorms.

A round, flat rock in the middle of the river was perfect for sitting on while lathering up. Then I would slip slowly down into the icy cold water and flail my arms furiously to rinse the suds off my goose-bump body.

Charlotte Plantz

One especially hot, sunny day, I set out for my afternoon bath. The pinching goose was always out in the yard, ready to lunge at us, but that day he didn't attack. He followed me to the river with all the other fowl straggling in a long line behind him. My heart began to beat a little faster as we approached my bathing rock. I thought of how vulnerable I would be sitting there naked to the world should somebody happen by. But something made me go on as though nothing unusual was happening.

As I positioned myself on the rock, legs pulled up, leaving nothing to chance, I was slightly amused, and then horrified when all the geese and ducks waded into the river and began to swim around and around my rocky perch. The pinching goose and I kept our eyes locked on one another, and the swimming went on and on. It was a mesmerizing experience, and I have to admit I loved the drama of it, even knowing I might get a mean pinch before it ended. Very slowly, I began to lather my limbs, and then torso, all the while eyes locked on the goose. As I slid down into the water I was astounded to see all the water birds begin their own bathing ritual. While paddling around me, they dipped their wings down into the water and then scooped the water up and over their bodies.

That day, following their lead, I didn't flail my arms, but dipped my cupped hands down into the water and then up over my body. We bathed together like that for what seemed like a long time. And then, suddenly it was over. While I dried my body with a towel, the birds shook their wings, spraying water all over one another until their feathers were dry. We all stepped out of the river, with me wrapped in a towel in the lead. The geese and ducks followed me back to the house, and I turned to thank them for sharing their baths with me. The pinching goose and I looked at one another as I passed by him to the steps. From that day forward he never chased any of us again. Or made any attempt to pinch. When the girls heard my story, they were impressed.

After spending five nights on the hard wooden bed platform, Julie, Sean, and I agreed something had to be done-soon. Murray, with a grocery list from Cathy, hiked over from their place, a distance of a mile or so (as the ravens flew) to join us on a trip to town in search of some kind of padding for our aching bodies. We stopped in Mora to take advantage of Pando's Laundromat, located in an adobe building that tilted toward the front. It was a recent addition to the slowly declining business section of town.

It was sad to see so many ancient adobe buildings lining both sides of the two-lane state highway falling into ruin. Directly across the road from Pando's stood Sanchez' Store, with plate glass windows so covered with red dust you could hardly see in or out. If it hadn't been for a sign in the window declaring the store open, we would have passed right by and missed out on a great experience. Inside the store, erect and dignified, with his white hair and goatee, we found Mr. Sanchez behind the counter.

Behind him were rows of shelves lined with canned goods. I was amazed by one shelf full of gallon cans of blue-and-white-labeled Morrell Lard. I couldn't imagine that much lard in one place, but then, I didn't know the cooking and eating habits of the Mora Valley.

The next surprise came when I noticed a young hippie woman standing slightly behind Mr. Sanchez. She introduced herself as Cindy and offered to help us with our needs. Mr. Sanchez smiled and began to question our names and presence in the high mountain community of his birth. During that era, most of the people of the Mora

Charlotte Plantz

Valley were not just friendly, but curious about outside Anglos who wished to live among them.

The people of the valley had lived in relative obscurity for centuries, except for the steady stream of Texans who drove back and forth on the little highway during their summer migration from the oppressive heat of the plains to the cool heights of the Sangre de Cristo Range. Had we spoken with a Texas drawl, we wouldn't have been as welcome in their community. We laughed at the huge billboard near the La Cueva turnoff that declared in big block letters: TEXANS GO HOME. You could tell by the faded paint that the sign had been there a long time.

None of us were discouraged by those words because we were from California. To us, Texas seemed like another country. And that was long before we started seeing CALIFORNICATE signs spring up. We new arrivals were acting out of some weird manifest destiny that had a driving force of its own. For some strange reason, the locals allowed us to stay, even when Mike and Murray started hearing stories about others who had been driven out. It was a curious time to be sure. And it was about to get curiouser and curiouser.

While we were loading dirty clothes into the machines, the afternoon monsoon was building up over the valley. We could hear the first rumbles of thunder. Mr. Pando said he would keep an eye on our laundry while we all went exploring for something soft to sleep on. Murray could be a real asset when depending on fate to provide all your needs, so we enlisted his help in finding some sort of padding for our bruised, weary bodies. The boy was like a fine hunting dog, his nostrils quivering slightly, all of his senses finely tuned toward the need at hand. He seemed to produce a special aura that would attract the object in one form or another. Since we

Me and My Magical Life

had first met him, our family had watched him pull one rabbit after another out of a hat.

In that small, dying community we were still feeling hopeful, and with keen eyes, we were in high spirits as we divided shopping lists and set off. Driving in, we had passed a store that looked to be in renovation. A large sign in the window declared the place to be a craft shop, so we headed in that direction.

Just then, a huge thunderclap let loose and a gigantic bolt of lightning struck almost immediately, letting us know the storm was right over the town of Mora. We scattered and ran for our lives, seeking any shelter available. I jumped into a recessed doorway of an old adobe building just as the rain came down in torrents. I was surprised to find Murray already taking up a good portion of the shelter, and we laughed at the coincidence.

As we pulled ourselves back into the recess, I noticed a small handwritten sign in the window advertising a few items for sale. The first two items listed were as follows: "1 single mattress: $5." The second item: "1 double mattress: $10." Murray and I were howling with laughter as we opened the door and entered the building.

It was no wonder people allowed us to stay in their valley; we were always laughing. Northern New Mexicans have a reputation for their humor and high awareness of magic in life. We particular outsiders must have touched something in their hearts and souls. At that moment, the mattress sales cinched it for us.

Murray's aura attracted the attention of an old woman who moved toward the door, inviting us in. She said her name was Alice, and we were in her store. It was in the process of becoming a craft center for local artists. Alice was gorgeous; a youthful look contrasted with her silver hair, and her eyes sparkled like the first evening stars. She told us of her project to market local crafts to tourists, and never stopped smiling as she continued to paint a counter bright Prussian blue. Alice invited us to look in a back room to view an array of mainly religious themed art that would soon be displayed in her new gallery.

After more conversation, we could feel that a bond had formed among the three of us. I couldn't decide whether we had captured Alice, or she had captured us. We nearly forgot the mattresses, and before we left we learned that Alice was 85 years old and quite eccentric. Over time, that bit would become significant. Once again, Julie, Cyndi, and Sean were amazed when we returned to Pando's and they heard our story of the lightning bolt that sent us to the right doorway. From that night to the end of our summer adventure, we slept like babes on the softness of our find.

It was time to establish a routine for our survival process. By then the girls had become aware of their roles, and wood gathering became the major activity for the three of them. The next big hurdle for me was the pile of rotten wood in back of the house. It was time to take hold of the rusted axe and chop away at the daunting pile. No sooner had I taken a firm grip on the axe handle than the entire head fell off onto the ground. I stood in disbelief, feeling tears beginning to well up, but I was determined not to show any weakness in front of my daughters. Instead, I picked up the axe-head and handle and got in the car and drove to Barry's for guidance. Their place was around two miles from us by road, the first mile on pavement. Once you turned off onto the dirt road you had to time it with the arrival of afternoon thunderstorms, or you could find yourself sliding around in gooey muck or not moving at all. We learned a lot about monsoons that summer.

The McWilliams clan had apparently entered into a conspiracy to provide as little help as possible for my survival-training program. They all agreed the axe-head needed a new edge, so Mike led me to a deteriorating blacksmith shed behind the house. The shed was filled with remnants of another time, and he pointed out a file, adding, "It may take a while, but you can probably get the job done." I said, "If I can't get it done we won't eat, because we won't have wood for the stove."

Mike looked at me with a smile tinged with pity. After examining the axe, he determined that the handle needed to be soaked in water overnight and then wedged back into the ax-head. He laughed and said he would help me this time, so we wouldn't starve. He said he would also clean the head and sharpen the edge for me. At the first rumble of thunder, I jumped in the car and headed back down the dirt track to the paved road before I got caught in the muck.

You cannot really appreciate thunderstorms until you experience one in Northern New Mexico. According to local meteorologists, the area has the second-highest lightning strike area in the country after Naples, Florida, so you could be assured of a heart-stopping experience just about every afternoon during summer. An anomaly to the area, are storms with torrential rain on one side of the road and dazzling sunshine on the other. It's possible to drive along a wall of hail or pouring rain and not get wet.   Years later we drove into Chacon Valley with a full moon on one side of the valley and a raging snowstorm on the other.

One reason for these phenomena is the proximity of the two mountain ranges that form the narrow valley.

Charlotte Plantz

Reaching up to 10,000 feet elevation, the two ranges often create their own weather. We once witnessed two different storms over both sides of the valley, with another forming at the headland. Thunder and lightning on those occasions made you take stock of your life. However, it was a thrilling experience.

The next morning, I saw Mike from the kitchen window hiking along the mountainside with my axe slung over his shoulder. Coffee was still hot on the wood cookstove, and because I had been experimenting with baking in the wood-fired oven, I was able to offer him something sweet, a bit of payment for his repair work. We carried our coffee and muffins out to the rough wood porch, where the intense summer sun warmed us thoroughly and lulled us into quiet now and then between conversations. The drone of honeybees at the wild roses was the only other sound, except for the murmur of the little river below. It was so incredibly beautiful and peaceful. For a while, the rest of the world ceased to exist. Suddenly, the silence was broken by the sound of tinkling bells, and then the sound of a harmonica.

One of the Cordova boys came into view from up above us. He was driving a herd of sheep down from the high meadows, called vegas. As the boy and his horse passed by, he smiled and waved and resumed his playing, thoroughly secure in his silent world high above the plains. Mike and I were speechless as we sat watching the scene play out before us. We were grateful for the opportunity to be there as witnesses to a very ordinary event in that timeless place. Finally, we roused ourselves and headed out to my pitiful woodpile. There was a log for cutting on, and Mike placed the first piece of scrap wood over it and gave it a whack with the newly sharpened axe-head. He was satisfied with the result, and turned to me and asked, "Are you ready to learn the art of woodcutting?" The woodcutter showed me how to hold the axe and swing, using centrifugal force to do the real work.

Mike watched me for a while to be sure I had the knack of it. He looked at the building clouds and said he should be heading back before the rain started, adding, "I don't want to interfere with your survival experience." The guy then left me to face the test of my newest survival skill. Actually, I was a little peeved that he wouldn't stay and chop some of the damned wood for us. Mike didn't seem like a very chivalrous type of guy. I chopped at the wood with an axe-head honed with anger and was amazed some time later by the results. When the girls came back from the Abeytas' they were impressed and eager to help me stack it in the back room for future use.

5
A Cast of Characters

When a few people have gathered together from around the country, and they appear to be having great fun and adventure, they are bound to attract other people of like minds and spirits. So it was not too strange when other folks began showing up on various dirt roads throughout the summer. The first ones arrived while I was in the outhouse at Barry and Cathy's. I heard Murray shouting my name. He was announcing that I had visitors, so it was with some excitement that I hurried out the rough wood door to find my old boss, Pat Dutra from Half Moon Bay, standing there in the debris-strewn yard. Next to Pat was her old friend Arlene from the same little town.

I shouldn't have been surprised to see them because I had been writing Pat regaling her with the beauty and adventure of the Chacon Valley. I had touched something in my friend that spurred her into action and led her to the end of the last dirt road in the narrow valley. I hadn't realized how close to the surface Pat's own sense of adventure lay. We hugged, made introductions all around, and then laughed over the two women driving on and upward as they left the paved road to search for me on the high, wild mountainside.

Pat and Arlene could hardly believe their eyes at the panorama that lay stretched out below them. The women assured me that I had not even begun to exaggerate the truth. It was a stroke of luck that the women found me at Barry and Cathy's, for when I had written I had not yet moved into my own little adobe, so could not give them directions. The drama of the McWilliams dwelling far surpassed that of any other place in the valley. Part of that was due to the abandoned village that peeked up from an even higher location on the mountainside. Our shared landlord, Pedro, had been born there in Las Colonias, a village that went back more than one hundred years.

We three women walked up behind the house a distance until we could see the adobe buildings that made up the village. The largest was the old schoolhouse, with windows around the four sides. We stood trying to imagine what life had been like for the children attending school in that remote and beautiful place. If Pedro Abeyta was an example, the others must have grown into adulthood with the same sense of peace and serenity. The three of us stood gazing at the empty ghost village for a while, each of us lost in our own thoughts until finally Pat said, she and Arlene wanted to take me out for a meal to celebrate their success in actually finding their destination. We laughed at the thought of a convenient restaurant from that vantage point, but I assured them that good New Mexican food could be had at Teresa's Café fifteen miles down the road to Mora.

By then, fifteen miles seemed like nothing, so we hiked down to the house for goodbyes and headed off down the rutted dirt track to the paved road and beyond to a chile feast. Having the women turn up in my life just then gave me a feeling of strength and courage. They were no-nonsense types who saved praise for extraordinary feats, and over the course of our drive and meal, they assured me that I was on the right track. By then, I needed all the positive reinforcement I could get.

Me and My Magical Life

On a brilliant, warm afternoon, I was hard at cleaning house, my mind awhirl with thoughts of life and how we all fit into the scheme of things. I had moved out onto the porch where the broom was flying across rough wooden steps when suddenly a guy came around the west corner of the house. He was holding a book in his hand. He was a wild-looking character, with dark hair sticking out all around his head, and he looked like a hippie.

We saw a lot of those around the Mora Valley, but not so many in the Chacon area. I was more than surprised, especially because my little adobe sat nearly by itself, a quarter of a mile from the road below. An arroyo ran between my house and another on the other side, but it had been closed up for years. There was another house about 150 yards south of ours, but it also looked as though it was empty. It wasn't. Pedro told us that a bunch of hippies lived there but they were in Texas for a while.

As the young man approached, he introduced himself as Randy and told me he lived up the canyon at the far end of the valley. He said he didn't own a car so was used to walking up and down the valley. Randy said he liked to hike way up to the meadows to lie in the green grass and contemplate life. I laughed, saying I had been doing the same thing, though with a broom in my hands.

I got us something cold to drink and we sat down on the porch. For some reason, I just began asking a million questions about life that had been rumbling around my brain for days. Randy looked at me thoughtfully, and then at the book he was holding. He passed the book over to me and I saw the title: The Book. The author was Alan Watts.

I vaguely recognized the author because of Murray, who was forever reading esoteric books and passing information my way. Randy and I chatted a while, watching the afternoon buildup of cumulus clouds, always a gorgeous sight. The young man said he needed to head home before the rain caught him unprepared. He said I could keep the book. I took the book inside and sat down on the couch and read it from cover to cover before the girls returned from their latest adventure. The Book: On the Taboo Against Knowing Who You Are answered every question I had been pondering over the past few days.

For days, Sean and my daughters had been exploring all the surrounding terrain, splashing in the icy river water, hiking up to the mountaintops, and especially visiting the Abeyta girls. The family included them on trips to Las Vegas and Mora and to a rodeo on the Fourth of July. A few times they were invited to dances where the Abeyta sons' band played. In July on a full moon night, the Abeyta girls took my girls to the river to wait for La Llorona, the legendary woman who had lost her little child to drowning in the river. Each full moon night, the story goes, La Llorona roams up and down the rivers, wailing for her lost child. On this night, Joseph and John Abeyta were hiding beneath the wooden bridge. Just when it grew very quiet, the boys jumped out shrieking, scaring the girls half to death.

The brothers were great storytellers and they would often accompany their father to our house in the evenings with large cans of water for our use. The well behind the house had become contaminated when a calf fell in and drowned the year before.

On those evenings, we sat around the living room, spellbound by the stories. Pedro and Joseph often alternated in the telling as one and then the other related different parts of the same story nearly seamlessly.

Me and My Magical Life

They told about watching beavers at their dams during full moon nights, and seeing wild turkeys fly up into tall trees to roost. Pedro told stories about saving cows during blizzards and drought, and being especially watchful of calves, that were tasty to coyotes. One story impressed us with Pedro's ingenuity in getting a cow out of a cattle guard. The wise old man gently talked the steer into standing still on the narrow metal crosspiece, one leg at a time until he had all four legs up. Our new friend also told us how, at five feet tall, he cut down strategic pine trees to the perfect height so he could stand on them in order to mount his tall horse.

One of the funniest stories Pedro ever told me was a long time later, when I took a turkey carcass to their place. I had asked whether chickens would eat the remains. Pedro told me a long story about chickens and their feeding habits, ending with the fact that they will eat anything. He pointed toward their feeding area, which was located behind a big wild rose bush, and I headed off in that direction. As I stepped around the bush, I nearly fainted on the spot. The chickens were feeding on a coyote carcass that John had found. When I returned to the house Pedro was laughing so hard he could hardly stand up. I had to sit down on the porch to grasp the irony of what I had just witnessed as Pedro reminded me that his chickens would eat anything! We never tired of hearing stories from everyone in the Abeyta family.

Sometime in mid-July, I heard the roar of engines coming up the mountain. I stepped out onto the porch to see who it might be. To my amazement, it was not on my road, but on the little dirt track to the south of us. There in a line were two cars and a motorcycle crossing the worst plank bridge I had ever seen. I was certain that by the third vehicle the planks would simply fold up on themselves and the car would fall into the Mora River. As people disembarked from the vehicles, they saw me and waved. They were hippies all right. I had never seen so much hair, even from where I stood. It was hard to tell, but I thought I saw two women and three men go into the green stucco house. Pedro had told us that locals called it the Texas house because the owner lived in Texas. And only a Texan would have a green stucco house in Chacon. All the houses in Chacon carried names or descriptions of present or past tenants.

By the next day, a couple of horses appeared out of nowhere in a rough corral near the house. By then, Julie and Sean showed growing interest in our new neighbors, because at that stage in their lives, they were especially interested in horses. It wasn't long before one of the new neighbors came for an introduction. He said his name was Paul and he invited us over to meet the others. We were astounded to walk into that Texas house and find pillows and cushions strewn all over the floor, surrounding a big, low, round table in the middle of the room. It was a hippie pad. They had a great record collection, and music poured out from huge speakers in two corners of the living room. It was almost as surprising as finding chickens feeding on a coyote.

The residents introduced themselves to us: Tony, a Levi's salesman who wore a wig of short hair when he set off on his motorcycle to sell Levi's jeans in Texas. His girlfriend, Murietta, appeared to be quite exotic. Then there was Ron and his lady, Lola Mae, and Paul, the handsome young guy. They were all natives of Texas, living their back-to-the-land-trip. Tony supported the group and the others maintained the house, garden, and horses.

Me and My Magical Life

When Tony returned after a selling trip, they would party until his next departure.

It was a pretty foreign group and setting for a bunch of females from suburban California, especially as next-door neighbors. My girls were thrilled when asked whether they would like to ride horses, and that determined the direction of their attention for the remaining summer. Murray and the others laughed their heads off as I described our new neighbors and their hippie pad. There was never much of an exchange between the two groups, and I suspected that the Texas group was a bit too theatrical even for the McWilliams clan. But I lucked out because Tony insisted on decking me out in the latest Levi's styles, at cost! Suddenly, in the middle of nowhere, I had become a fashionista

6
The dinner Party and The End of a Magic Summer

The sound of a car caught my attention and I ran to the window in time to see Barry's old blue Dodge pickup grinding up the last grade from the bridge. Beowolf and Mary Ann, the McWilliams dogs, were doing the two-step in the truck bed trying to maintain their footing. The only relief they had was on the half-mile stretch of pavement before the turnoff at Pedro's. That day the clay roads were dry, though the ruts appeared somewhat deeper than usual. The afternoon rains were actually cloudbursts, great white cumulus clouds that roared in with the speed of a freight train.

The clouds piled on top of one another at the end of the valley, pushing, bumping, and shoving until soon, the entire valley was covered. The great white billows began to smooth out, stretching themselves to a tight gray mantle, and then they would suddenly explode, showering the land with billions of life-giving drops. A network of dirt roads seemed to lie in submission, waiting for the afternoon onslaught. Today's ruts filled, melted, and smoothed out and dried quickly before the next storm wreaked its havoc.

Barry had lured us to Chacon with his romantic impressions. He had a special talent for painting pictures so vivid and exciting that grown men had been known to up and quit a secure job in order to race to "the most beautiful, unique place on earth" of the moment. Within a thirteen-year period, Barry had moved twelve times, and the letters were always the same. He usually managed to find a place at the end of the last dirt road in the most remote corner of any given state or county. This is a positive description of our friend, for wherever he settled, even though briefly, you could be sure the place would be breathtakingly beautiful, and the people friendlier than most you had met. The experience was guaranteed to leave an imprint forever.

Cathy, Barry's wife, had become adept at dismantling or setting up a household on a moment's notice. She could turn out gourmet meals on a woodstove, coax vegetables from a hurriedly planted garden, and pack tiny children out on a horse after a blizzard. The woman had a voice like an angel and was able to entertain herself with song writing and poetry. Because of her talents and serene disposition, Cathy maintained her sanity during long periods of isolation. When Barry wasn't teaching school or breaking horses, he was sometimes known to sit still long enough to write a story, invent a game, or draw thought-provoking cartoons.

"Howdy," Barry said, stomping dirt off his boots. "I just came up to invite you to a dinner party tomorrow night. Do ya think your girls would keep Colin here for the evening?" Colin was almost three years old, a red-haired, cherubic dynamo who loved Hoyt Axton music. He was a pint-size package of his dad's energy.

"The girls are out hiking. I'll check with them when they get back, but I'm sure they won't mind," I replied. By then I was getting excited at the thought of an organized dinner party.

Me and Mt Magical Life

"Only one thing needs taking care of to make this dinner a success," mused Barry, as I noticed him trying to formulate words for the proper effect. "Well, ya see, I need twenty dollars to buy the steaks. If you'd be willing to buy my old record player for the twenty dollars, seeing as how you didn't bring a radio, I'd be willing to lend you some records. And I'll probably have some money by the time you leave at the end of summer so I could actually buy it back from you." Words tumbled out in a well-thought-out stream.

I didn't need to say that I would be willing to kick in the twenty without the record player, but that wasn't the point. Barry and I concluded a transaction that felt strangely satisfying. We worked out details for everyone's role the following evening. Barry whistled for his dogs. They had been out chasing cows and were ready for the drive as they rattled off down the dirt road toward home.

My girls were happy for the diversion that was Colin, in fact, to the point of suggesting that they keep him overnight. They encouraged me to spend the night at Barry and Cathy's in case it rained, giving them an added sense of responsibility, edged with a touch of adventure. We all seemed to be caught up in the spirit of individual survival skills. The girls were feeling very adult at thirteen and sixteen, while I felt like a kid who had just been given permission to have a sleepover at a friend's house. I had never spent a night away from my family, unless it had been to a hospital or a few runs to Half Moon Bay for art shows. It was another new adventure for us all.

Cathy arrived the next evening with Colin. The two of us were feeling almost giddy with excitement. We had shared many meals together over the summer, but that evening felt special. Two storms that had been building since afternoon rumbled softly in the distance.

Charlotte Plantz

The air was strangely soft and warm, creating an environment of hushed sounds. We found ourselves talking in lower tones than normal. What really made it special was that the men had taken complete charge of the meal. Mike had built a barbecue pit and was preparing charcoal to a level of glowing perfection.

By the time we reached the house, Murray was up to his armpits in flour. Actually, the entire kitchen was up to Murray's armpits in flour, as he coaxed a stiff ball of dough into a flat tortilla. "Hot damn," he shouted as we entered the hazy room. "How does Bessie Abeyta whip out a couple dozen of these things every morning?" Beads of perspiration were forming on Murray's upper lip as Cathy and I backed out the door, trying not to laugh at his serious labor. Barry was in the garden picking lettuce and pulling up tiny green onions and plump red radishes. The vegetable had to be zucchini. I had never seen so much zucchini.

The garden was a wonder at that altitude. A small acequia, or irrigation ditch, ran down from a spring. The water had been sidetracked through the garden and back out to the ditch, where it traveled on to the next ranch to be used in the same way. When Pedro and Bessie lived there, he had kept a garden hose next to the acequia where he tapped into the water. The hose lay outstretched in the sun during the morning hours, warming the water to the right temperature.

Pedro chuckled as he told us, "That hose holds just the right amount of water for a quick afternoon shower." Pedro had dug a well shortly before they moved down to their new house on the paved road, so Barry and Cathy had cold running water in their kitchen. In the new house, for the first time in their lives, the Abeyta family had indoor plumbing. Circa 1972, they were among the first of their neighbors to enjoy that luxury.

Me and Mt Magical Life

Cathy and I felt somewhat useless as we wandered aimlessly around. Finally we settled on picking a big bouquet of wildflowers for the table. Suddenly, we heard a bloodcurdling scream. Cathy and I raced through the meadow to find Mike, red in the face, arms flailing, screaming at Barry to get away from his barbecue. Barry had tried to be helpful while Mike was getting something from the kitchen; he had picked up one of the two-pound steaks to turn it-and dropped it on the ground.

The air of festivity hung by a thread. In a moment it passed. All of us were determined that nothing would spoil our dinner party. Everything was ready. Thunder sounded a drum roll as the first golden rays of evening hurled themselves over the mountain, casting a shimmer about the valley. Cathy was sure Zeus was sitting on the Jicarita Peak summit, observing the scene below, now and then tossing out a handful of colorful rays. It was easy to visualize that from where we sat.

The meal could almost be anticlimactic if it weren't for the drama that was taking place all around us. The storms continued to move in slowly on the little valley, which was unusual. After stuffing ourselves to the waddle stage, we adjourned to sit on a haystack behind the house. From that vantage point it was possible to scan the entire valley. The aspens across the way were just beginning to turn color: pale yellows and occasionally a hint of orange peeked through the mass of green.

We could hear a dog bark two miles down the valley. Zeus continued his creative game, throwing rays of pink, mauve, and purple, along with red, orange, and a dozen shades of gold. The orchestration continued as the beat of the storms began to pick up. All at once, huge raindrops began to fall ever so slowly.

Charlotte Plantz

Mike and Murray ran down the mountainside while Cathy, Barry, and I sat watching them grow smaller and smaller. They were leaping and twirling in the freshly mown hay meadows, surely growing drunk on the smells of newly cut grass. High above the dancing figures, we were getting our own high from the smell of rain and damp earth.

Just as suddenly as it had begun, the rain stopped. However, the lightning and thunder continued in the most delicate way imaginable. We could hear Mike and Murray blowing blades of grass over their thumbs, giving birdcalls. Zeus had grown tired of his game. One final burst of rays and it was over. Darkness descended over the valley, but we couldn't move. The night was so warm, so electric and intoxicating, we all knew it must be experienced to the end.

No sounds came from the other haystack where Murray and Mike had landed. Barry, Cathy and I sat in absolute silence, absorbing the storm. All of a sudden we heard music, guitar music, so haunting that we felt goose bumps. Mike had silently slipped back to the house in the dark and fetched his guitar. A flash of lightning illuminated the guitar player sitting on the woodpile near the house. He was playing to the storm. None of us had ever heard Mike play like that; it was as though he was inspired by the energy of the night.

Another bolt of lightning brought our focus to Murray, who was dancing around the haystack to the rhythm of the guitar. It was hard to tell whether the storm had become music or the music had become storm. It all seemed to merge with the moment. Suddenly, as the music whipped the storm into a frenzy, there was a gigantic thunderclap, a huge bolt of lightning, and then, total silence. None of us would ever forget that dinner party.

Me and Mt Magical Life

The dinner party turned out to be a going-away party for us. We had been so busy that we failed to notice summer was drawing to a close. It was time for us to pack up and head west. The day before we were to leave, Mike walked through a drizzle to say goodbye. The two of us had become good friends, and he wanted me to know that he would be there for me as I dealt with all that lay ahead of me. I was deeply touched by his sincerity. Mike's friendship gave me a feeling of comfort at just the right time in my life.

As clouds continued to build, Julie, Cyndi, Sean, and I walked down to say goodbye to the Abeyta family. We thanked them for all they had done for us in our time there. Bessie and I had become quite close, especially as she had been privy to some of my phone calls to my spouse. She understood from the tone of my voice what was happening in my life. Without offering comment, my friend was able to convey her compassion for my situation.

We promised to stay in contact and she wanted me to know that my little adobe house would be there for me any time I needed it.

Amazingly, ten years later I would find myself back in that house, but under very different circumstances. Bessie, Pedro, and their children agreed that it had indeed been a "magic summer." Ten years later they would tell me there had never been another one like it.

The girls and I drove down the little dirt road for the last time. And none too soon, for a deluge was about to hit the valley. We would have been stuck for days in the little adobe house until the muddy road dried out. We were a quiet group for many miles as each of us relived the events of summer. We had become more mature and resourceful, patient and considerate than we had been at the beginning of our adventure. The end of summer would actually become the beginning of a new life for me and my daughters and their friend.

Twelve hundred miles later as I drove into our driveway, there was no doubt in my mind about what I needed to do. My husband knew it the moment I walked through the door, and I think it was a relief for us both. The pretense was over. The marriage was over. And it didn't take long for me to put a plan into action. I had wasted too many years trying to make it work. The first thing I did was to sit down with my daughters and include them in my plan. They were old enough to make some decisions for themselves.

Their father had always been a great parent and they adored him. Because he had always undermined my decisions about parenting, my daughters thought of me as far more strict than their dad. He was a pushover in their eyes, a great asset for a teenager. Julie decided she wanted to join me in returning to New Mexico. Cyndi was especially close to her father, so she chose to stay with him.

The year was 1972, when many women were feeling the need to stand up for themselves. In a moment of anger, my husband had found our marriage license and waved it in the air, shouting, "This paper says you belong to me. I own you." No wonder we were in rebellion. My own father had said as much ten years earlier, when I should have left my husband. I could hardly believe the strength I now felt.

Nothing would stop me from breaking free of the bondage I felt. Not money, not security, not disownment by my own family. For me, it was a matter of life and death, sanity over insanity, a chance for happiness and creative fulfillment. I knew then that at the end of my life, I wouldn't have to say, "Damn, what was I thinking?"

Once I made the announcement that I was leaving, I had to figure out how to make it happen-on four hundred dollars. I had money for gas to drive somewhere, but not enough for a car. In my deepest parts, I knew there was a way back to New Mexico. And then Murray called to see how we were doing. When I filled him in on the situation, he nearly shouted, "Wow, I just got back from my folks', and my dad gave me his old pickup. I could come and get you and Julie." And that is what he did. Of course, my soon-to-be-ex-husband would tell everyone that I had run off with a hippie kid. The truth was, I gratefully accepted a ride out of the state and a bad marriage. At that point, I would have accepted a ride in a donkey cart.

When Fr Chris heard about the trip, he asked to ride along with Murray for company. We had met at Pancho's Laundromat in Mora earlier during our Chacon stay. My soon-to-be seventeen-year-old daughter, Julie, and I drove off with young Murray and the black monk. All four of us were packed in the cab of his truck, something that would now be illegal. From Sacramento, to celebrate, we decided to head to San Francisco for Chinese food, a two-hundred mile, out-of-the-way detour. Dear old friends in El Granada, south of San Francisco, took us in for the night and wished us well the next morning as we headed east for an entirely new life. At that point I no longer possessed a house key, car key, or checking account. Credit cards in a woman's name were unheard of at the time. It didn't occur to me that Julie and I could not survive on the four hundred dollars in my pocket. Only time would tell.

7
Highlands University Student

The day after Julie, Murray, Fr Chris, and I arrived back in Northern New Mexico I knew I had to find work immediately, even though I was aware that San Miguel County had the second-highest unemployment level in the country. For a very long time the area had been considered an official poverty area. Knowing all the facts did not bother me in the least. My level of optimism had a way of reaching extreme heights in tight situations. We were staying with Barry and Cathy until we found a place, so Julie and I talked Murray into driving us to Las Vegas. We were two days separated from our former life as a family, but we were simply too excited to be frightened.

On the other hand, Murray was a wreck. The drive seemed to have a grip on his tongue until finally he could barely spit out, "Charlotte, you can't possibly live with only four hundred dollars to your name. You'll never find a place to live, and how do you ever expect to find a job in this God-forsaken place, let alone support two people?"

By the time we hit town I had had enough. I said to Murray, "Please pull over." He brought the pickup to a halt, and I looked him squarely in the eyes and calmly ordered him to get out. Reluctantly, he did get out at a little park, and I slid over to the driver's side.

Charlotte Plantz

Without saying another word, Julie and I knew that if we were going to survive, it would have to be on our own energy.

To reinforce our positive attitude, the first stop we made was at Safeway, where we bought groceries. The next stop was at Highlands University, where Julie decided to sit on the lawn with a book while I set forth to convince the personnel people of my worth as a potential employee. The next few hours were rather exceptional. When I had filled out an application and turned it over to a woman at the counter, some sort of strange bond was formed between us. As she read over the application, she made little sounds of "hmm," occasionally looking up at me. Finally she asked, "How long have you been separated from your husband?"

"Two days," I replied.

She smiled, reading on, and then said, "Something about you makes me feel that you should be back in school."

"Oh, I can't afford that luxury now," I cried. "Four hundred dollars won't last very long for two people."

The woman was adamant as she began writing on small slips of paper. She handed two of those to me and said, "Take this one to the admissions office, and the other to the financial aid office. I have written directions on the back. School begins Monday, but I think there is still time to get you accepted and enrolled."

Obediently, and a little numb, I found my way to the beginning of a new life. The people at admissions were waiting for me, and I was immediately ushered into the dean's office. The middle-aged gentleman was like a patient, gentle father, eager to encourage some latent offspring in the value of higher education. The room took on a warm, secure feeling, lulling me into a rosy world of unlimited possibilities.

Me and My Magical Life

A while later, I floated out of the office with an appointment for Saturday, the official day of my acceptance. From there, I headed to financial aid, where the staff also had been alerted to my existence. I was offered a fifteen-hours-a-week work-study that paid one hundred seventeen dollars a month for working in the admissions office. Three hours after entering the front door of Highlands University, I found myself as a full-time student, with a part-time job.

Julie and I had three days to find a place to live, but I somehow knew we would find it that very day, even if the little city of fifteen thousand felt packed to the hilt with college students. The majority of the three thousand students were Hispanic and young, coming from remote areas throughout the state, eager for a few adventures without the ever-present parental figures looming over them. At that time, there were few dorms, and hardly any of the students wanted to live on campus, so housing in town was especially tight. Knowing that that did not daunt me at all.

Julie could hardly believe her ears as my story unfolded. We celebrated with a picnic on the lawn of the little university and then simply walked around the block to where our new friend, Alice, whom we had met earlier that summer, lived, right across the alley from the men's dorm. I rang the bell and felt greatly warmed by the greeting Alice extended. She was delighted to see us and insisted on tea and cookies to celebrate our return. We had not seen one another since the beginning of summer. Alice grew as excited as we were as I related the story of Highlands University. However, our excitement faded somewhat when she said she knew of nothing available to rent.

Charlotte Plantz

Just then, a young woman came in the house. She approached Alice, handing her a set of keys. "Well, I'm all moved. It was nice knowing you, Alice," she said, as we looked at one another in disbelief. Alice shook her head slowly, saying, "I must be getting old. There is a vacant apartment right upstairs in my own house."

Murray had fetched us from California because I no longer owned a car. Everything we owned was in the little camper on his truck. Julie and I were positively giddy as we ran back around the corner, laughing hysterically. The funniest part was we didn't even have to shop for food! It was late afternoon when we found Murray asleep on the park lawn. Julie and I feigned solemnity as we walked back to the truck, trying not to look at one another. Back at the wheel, I asked Murray to stop at Alice's as he continued his morning monologue of doom. When he pulled in front of the house, Julie said, "Murray, look in back of the truck." He turned to peer through the rear window. The truck was empty. His eyes were huge with disbelief.

We invited our driver up for a glass of wine to help christen our new home. Once he was inside, Murray fell on the little couch, howling with laughter upon seeing groceries in the cupboards. The guy could hardly contain himself when I handed him my admission slips and W-4 forms. After Murray calmed down, he looked at me intently and declared, "It never fails; housewives and nuns get all the breaks."

As our young friend drove away to carry news to our friends up the mountain that Charlotte and Julie would not perish after all, the reality of what I had done hit me. Not what I had done that day, but what I had done two days before. Julie and I looked at each other and burst into great racking sobs. She had no father. I had no husband. We had no family, for everyone had disowned us.

Me and My Magical Life

We howled and cried for what seemed like an eternity, and then cutting through all of our noise, a knock resounded at the door. We were half expecting our husband/father to be coming to drag us home. Quickly wiping away tears, I opened the door to Alice, who was holding a big platter of fried chicken. Her twinkly eyes took in the entire scene. She said, "Take this, and I will be right back with the rest." Alice moved slowly, so we had time to get ourselves together before she returned with bowls of mashed potatoes and corn. One more trip would produce an apple pie. Alice was in her glory as a religious woman, for she was witness to the looks on our faces as she literally brought us back from the brink of despair.

It had been a day of high drama, and as exhausted as we felt, it was wonderful being able to share it with someone special. Alice was an exceptional human being. She had lived most of her life in Las Vegas. She was a Christian Scientist and a widow of many years. Alice augmented her income with the three rental apartments upstairs. Our place was tiny, but ingeniously contrived to provide everything one might need. The kitchen was no bigger than a closet, but it was cheery and contained tons of cupboard space as if by magic. The living room held a tiny couch, buffet, chair, and tiny table with one leg affixed to a corner.

Windows all across the room looked out on a tree-rimmed parking lot belonging to the men's dorm. The bedroom was barely big enough for a single bed and dresser. The room, fortunately, contained a lot of built-in cupboards and a closet. The bathroom was nearly the biggest room in the house. Julie and I were to take turns sleeping on the floor of the living room. I learned a lot from that experience. It was a prelude to some of the worst beds in the world that I would encounter during my travels.

8
The Anniversary Mass

Not too long after Julie and I got settled into our little apartment I met Sister Joanna. We found ourselves in the same life drawing class and were drawn to one another because of age, and because we were like two fish out of water in that predominantly Hispanic school. Joanna stood out more than me because of her black robe and white wimple. She was short and round and because you couldn't see her feet, she appeared to be floating along the hallways.

It made us both smile when students did a double take and nearly bowed in front of her as a result of their Catholic heritage. The nun was working on a master's degree in iconography, and what the students didn't know was that Joanna belonged to a small sect of American Orthodox practitioners who lived and practiced in Mora. It wasn't long before the nun introduced Julie, Murray, and me to her peers.

Even though Fr Chris had been with us on the drive from California it slipped my mind until I met Joanna. She invited us to visit the little monastery they had set up in a green stucco house next to the highway in the middle of Mora. It was a very strange place for a group of religious "outsiders" to set up an American Orthodox monastery. Northern New Mexico at that time was predominantly and deeply Catholic. Penitentes still practiced their acts of penance that included self-flagellation. The sect of four devotees went about their daily business dressed in black robes and pillbox hats. We never heard locals discuss them at all. That was, until later.

When I met Fr Chris again it was as a student at Highlands. I had forgotten that he was black. Not that black was different, but being black in Mora was out of the ordinary. He did look like a monk, because of the coarse brown robe he wore. The 26-year-old had arrived from Chicago and worked on a master's degree in sociology at Highlands University during the week. On weekends, Fr Chris conducted American Orthodox rituals at the monastery in Mora.

One fall weekend, the two of us bumped into one another at an Equinox party at Adam Worker's hippie compound in La Sierra, high above the Mora Valley. The party went on into the evening and Fr Chris missed vespers. When word reached the bishop, Fr Chris was banned from seeing me again. The bishop thought me a bad influence on his resident monk, probably because I had been feeding the monk now and then when he was in town and talking about non-holy subject matter.

Fr David, the only priest at the monastery, was to me a reincarnation of Rasputin. His piercing eyes could look straight through you into your soul. He was tall, thirtyish, dark-skinned with black hair and a beard that he wore pointed. Adding to his overall appearance as Rasputin, Fr David wore a black pillbox hat of Greek origin and a long, flowing black cape, which he once used to create a scene of high-camp drama at the Safeway.

On this occasion, I was about to enter the store. As I stepped on the automatic door opener, the door flew open, revealing Fr David in his regalia. He flung the cape over one shoulder, while bellowing huskily, "Charlotte, I greet you." Everyone in the store stopped to stare as I hissed, "David, why can't you just say hello like everyone else?" Mike told me that Fr David invited him to drop by to look at his classical music and porn book collection. As time passed, gossip made its way up the little highway to Mora with more frequency.

Bishop Cunningham was English-Irish, fortyish, with a slight Oxford accent. He was tall and distinguished looking, with red hair and a neatly trimmed beard. He taught English at Mora High School, where everyone spoke Spanish as a way of life. He was the only one of the sect who lived at the monastery, and he kept his door open so students could drop in after school. The bishop ferried students to the Opera in Santa Fe during the summer and tried to set up a recreation center for local teens. And that's when people started talking about the group and their motives.

It turned out that all four members of the Orthodox sect were from Chicago. The group felt they had been called to Northern New Mexico for their missionary work. Their order worked in the public sector. They led celibate lives and devoted themselves to religious and social work. The sect had to provide for all their needs. There was no Mother Church, so parishioners and others donated things they needed. Samsonite (the luggage manufacturer) donated surplus suitcase lining material to be made into robes. A couple of local women sewed for the four of them, creating robes of different colors for special events, one of which we were invited to attend.

It was to be an anniversary mass for Fr Chris to celebrate his one-year anniversary as a monk. He personally invited Julie, Murray, and me to attend and

Charlotte Plantz

hoped we would honor his invitation. Murray and Julie were skeptical but curious. None of us were religious in the formal sense, but we did respect those who had chosen that path. We agreed to attend.

The monastery chapel was in a small cinderblock building attached to the green Texas house. The interior was painted a blinding white, with small Greek icon paintings lined up around the walls. A simple altar had been set up, and there were several crude benches lining the walls beneath the icons. The room was austere in its simplicity, but it did have a religious feel about it. The three of us sat quietly, glued in place and smiling nervously at one another now and then. Murray looked like he wanted to bolt, but checked himself.

In the back room, Fr Chris began the chanting that accompanied the service. The bishop entered first, in a robe of white satin brocade. He was wearing a tall, conical hat of white trimmed in gold. He carried a large gold crucifix on a chain, which he placed on the altar. Behind him, chanting, with his head held high, was Fr David. He was dressed in gold satin brocade and wore a pillbox hat. He swung a censer, a large golden ball containing incense. With each swing, little puffs of incense were released. Fr Chris was close behind, wearing a red brocade robe, swinging an identical censer. For me, the room was growing closer with each swing. Joanna arrived last, clad in a white brocade robe, the white wimple surrounding her plump, angelic face.

The group moved into position for the ceremony, bowing heads for the first prayer. I lowered my head, keeping my eyes open so I would be less likely to faint from all the incense. My eyes moved slowly across the floor, pausing here and there in search of something of interest. I looked at the bishop's feet, encased in proper

68

black English-type shoes. My eyes moved on to Fr David's cowboy boots. "Cowboy boots? With gold satin brocade?" I chuckled to myself. My eyes traveled on, now to Fr Chris. His bare feet were in monk-like sandals. I could feel a laugh beginning as I fought to maintain control. The incense made me feel like I might faint, and I tried not to look at Joanna's feet, as one foot exposed itself beneath her robe, but my eyes darted quickly to her shoe.

I knew instantly that I had to take flight. There, beneath the beautiful Samsonite-suitcase-lining white robe, appeared a black sneaker with white stripes. Julie and Murray were ready to lynch me over my behavior. I blamed it on the incense, and in a whisper convinced them it was either take flight or faint on the spot.

Following the service, the three of us joined the small congregation for a lovely anniversary meal. We thanked Fr Chris and his comrades for the invitation. Not too long after the mass, the American Orthodox group was driven out of the community. Our Chacon friends told us that people had begun to question the sect's presence, and rumors had begun to fly.

The Brown Power movement had recently become active in the area and questioned all Anglo outsiders' motives, riling up entire communities. That was the beginning of a very dark period for a while. If it hadn't been for the Abeyta family, we would probably have been run out too.

Alice became a regular part of our routine. When I became depressed, she knew almost instinctively. During those periods I would find slips of paper under my door containing poetry or words of wisdom. Perhaps a bit of philosophy or a quote from some book on Christian Science. We related as equals, each believing that the other was capable of outrageous feats. When Julie and I, on occasion, entertained guests in our little abode, Alice was usually invited. She thrived on the creative stimulation that quickly filled the small rooms. We valued her participation, grateful for her knowledge of local history and color.

Alice had made arrangements for the first show at her new gallery in Mora to be photography featuring work by Murray, Mike Plantz, Richard Atkinson, and Ray (the pig farmer) Lowe. The group of four had done a photographic essay on the people of the Mora Valley. The show would open in November and then travel to libraries throughout the state. Our little apartment became the center of activity because I had access to a dry-mount press, sorely needed for the framing process. The press was nearly as big as the living room, so you can imagine the chaos when four photographers showed up simultaneously with stacks of photographs to mount. Alice loved it! She became more and more animated as work for the show progressed.

As exam time rolled around, my life became more and more hectic. I worked part time evenings at a little print shop, was carrying a load of eighteen units, working fifteen hours, and trying to convince myself that although it had been eighteen years since I had been in school, it didn't necessarily mean I would fail every subject. As it turned out, I didn't fail even one class: five classes received A's and one a B. The B prompted me to ask for a tutor in earth science. My professor, Werner Muller, sent me Carl Cathy, a graduate geology student who was nearly my own age. It was he who urged me on to an A by the end of term.

Carl became a good friend, especially because I baked bread and cinnamon rolls every other Thursday morning, and the aroma wound down from my windows into the men's dorm. By the time I received the next A in earth science, Carl proposed marriage. He wanted to swoop me off to Lubbock, Texas, where he would save me from my bohemian friends and encourage me to become a lady geologist who would bake cinnamon buns for the rest of our natural lives.

I thanked Carl for his tutoring help and the marriage proposal, but convinced him that at last, I had actually found my own bohemian roots. He drove back to Lubbock, shaking his head at such thinking. That experience helped me become even more determined to find the right creative path for myself. It was such a relief to realize that I did not need a man to take care of me, in spite of my dire financial situation. Oddly, there I was, surrounded by a group of creative men, and all I wanted was to be part of the creative process.

Night after night, I was in the middle of my living room with three to four guys, working on the photography show with no thought of a relationship. Although just after Carl left, I did remark one night that I might be ready to date. The entire group looked at me and almost in unison said, "Not yet, Charlotte. You are not ready." As an afterthought, Mike said quietly, "I would like to take you out, but I don't have any money." I didn't have that thought again for months, until the idea of Mexico popped into my head.

By Halloween, our life was intense on the home front. Poor Julie was attending Robertson High School and dreading each day as she trudged through piles of autumn leaves on the sidewalks and streets of Las Vegas. As much as she enjoyed the aromas that accompanied the seasonal transition, she pined for old friends, and especially for her sister and father. By the time Julie had to plow through deep snow, her fantasy of life in Las Vegas with her mother began to unravel as quickly as a ball of yarn rolling across the floor.

As Thanksgiving drew closer, my daughter announced that she would return to Folsom to finish high school with her friends. My heart sank, but I didn't blame her for wanting to be with her peers. As she stated, "Mom, I'm about the only blond in the school, and I'm wearing hand-painted clothing, both of which make me stand out like a circus clown. I just don't fit here." The next day Julie went to the principal and thanked him for her experience at his school. She said goodbye and found a ride to Albuquerque, where she boarded a plane to Sacramento.

Two days later, Mike showed up at my apartment to say goodbye. He too was returning to California. Once the photography show had been hung, Mike took stock of his life. He was out of money, and reasoned that it was time to get back to a regular job and a bathtub. Winter was fast approaching, bringing about adjustments in everyone's lives.

Murray moved down from the mountains into a cabin twelve miles out of town. He too was attending the university, and we were in two of the same classes. Barry and Cathy, with whom Mike and Murray had been living all summer and fall, were getting their winter supply of wood chopped and stacked. Mike had spent weeks chopping, but it was a drop in the bucket compared to what was needed to survive a winter at that altitude.

Suddenly, it seemed that everyone who knew me was coming down from the mountains on Thursdays to take a bath at my place. One blustery day during an art class, a young woman dropped a jar of black paint on top of me while I was kneeling at my locker. I sprinted home to bathe. When I opened my door, the apartment was

Me and My Magical Life

filled with people waiting to use my bathroom. For a few moments I went berserk.

Alice was much more patient than me. She was paying the water bill, and I felt guilty and responsible for the growing problem. It came to a head one day when some people I barely knew came by to ask whether they might "borrow" my bathroom one day a week. My response was a resounding "No."

A rather odd though nice fellow, whom everyone called "weird Barry," called on me one afternoon. He had come, he said, to declare his love for me. He also asked whether he might move in with me. He also lived in the mountains and the first snow had just fallen. The more snow that fell, the more visitors and requests found their way to my door. Alice never mentioned all the traffic going up and down her stairs. Except for one time.

Murray had a new puppy, which he sneaked up the stairs to meet me. Alice heard the commotion and followed him up. We were caught with the goods. She gave us both a scathing lecture for breaking her ironclad rule of NO PETS, then, she carried the pup down to her place for a dish of warm milk. While the apartments of Alice shone with cleanliness, the house of Alice, below, was a disaster. Boxes were stacked along walls; furniture was piled on top of furniture. Debris was everywhere. The kitchen was something out of a horror story: cats walked around on counters, stove, table. There must have been six cats running Alice's life. Her greatest fear was that she might weaken, allowing tenants to infiltrate with animals. It was almost as though the upstairs part of her life represented calm and order. If she were to lose that, she would surely perish.

With Julie and Mike gone and the photography show about to travel around the state, I was pretty much alone except for my two new friends, Joanna, the nun, and the other, a young woman from Bangladesh named Halide Salaam. Like Joanna, Halide was also in a master's art program. None of us had a car, so we met for coffee now and then in the student center and attended concerts and plays as often as possible. Because it was an especially snowy winter, none of us ventured out very often.

One afternoon after my work at the admissions office, Joanna and I happened to meet on the sidewalk, which was very icy. We had to walk down a hill on our way home, and because we were having trouble standing upright, we began to run and slide. We were such a funny sight: Joanna, short and chubby and dressed in a black habit and big white wimple, and me, tall and thin, wearing Tony's discount designer Levi's jeans, sailing down the hill, shrieking with laughter. A couple of drivers stopped to laugh with us, for Las Vegans were known for their collective sense of humor.

With a drive only one-third the distance from Chacon, Murray became more a part of my daily life, especially since we shared classes three days a week. The poor kid was so stunned by my sense of loss over Julie leaving that he felt some sense of responsibility in watching over me. It turned out to be a comforting trade-off. Murray and Alice became my family, and we shared many meals at the tiny corner table.

At times, the boy filled my home with kid sounds; on other occasions we related on intellectual levels that surprised us both. Murray was definitely brilliant. He was also witty and charming, and fun to be with. Alice adored him. Without them, I doubt that I would have survived that winter. Never in my life had I been without family for Thanksgiving or Christmas, surely the most devastating times for anyone facing loneliness.

9
The Christmas Gift

In all the years of my life there had never been one without a Christmas tree-until that one. To me, a tree was one of the special things about the holiday season. I used to begin working on homemade ornaments at the beginning of November; not that they were anything spectacular, but they were creative. Our trees usually had a lot of character.

One year we cut the top of a jack pine on our property. When it was felled it proved to have only two branches: one very big set at the bottom with a lot of empty space in between that and the other set at the top. There was nothing much to trim, but being creative I saw a lot of potential-or so I told my family. That tree did take some ingenuity; it was decorated with one hundred plastic apples that I found for a penny apiece and fifty paper doves cut out of white construction paper. My young daughters filled in some of the blank spots with bird's nests they found in a field at the end of our street. Friends and neighbors dropped in to have a laugh at our tree, and for the next decade our trees attracted a lot of attention.

Fast-forward to Las Vegas, New Mexico, where a string of December snowstorms created a holiday atmosphere that compounded my misery of being alone for Christmas. My girls were spending the two-week holiday with their dad in California, the first time we had been apart for that long. My social life was down to Alice and Murray. Murray tried to convince me that to become a strong human being I should give up a Christmas tradition. Murray had a thing about sentimentality being bad for your health. It was already a year of shattered traditions. But he was right.

Christmas had been hanging over my head since the end of summer. I thought it strange that a season could play such havoc with my senses. I tried to shake off the thoughts and was determined to get through the holiday on my own. And I decided to take Murray's challenge and give up having a Christmas tree. At the admissions office where I worked, I announced to the staff that I was giving up the tree tradition, adding that my apartment was too small for a tree of any size. They all seemed to nod, averting their eyes as they turned away silently.

I had signed up to work as much as possible during the holiday season, but I felt the weight of the university being shut down for two weeks over Christmas. My friend Johanna returned to Chicago, and then Murray announced he was flying to Florida to be with his family for a couple of weeks. I knew that at some point in life, all of us find ourselves completely alone, either by choice or divine intervention. It must be my time to deal with that reality.

Loneliness in Las Vegas, New Mexico, was heightened by the absurdity of one radio station that came in clearly during the evening hours. The programming included the Rosary Hour from six p.m. to seven p.m., followed by local football or basketball games, depending on the season. After the game, if I was awake I would be

Me and My Magical Life

treated to a Top 40 music program. As Christmas drew closer I became familiar with all the players on the Highlands teams and memorized the Rosary. None of that, however, diverted my attention from a tree.

I walked downtown more frequently, making sure I had to pass all the tree lots. Old habits die slowly, but I tried to stay on track. The day before school shut down, the office manager begged me to take a little decorated tree that had been sitting on the counter. Peggy had become concerned with my life, and I knew it would be a relief for her if I took the tree so she could enjoy her own Christmas tree free of concern. I thanked Peggy, but by then was determined to see the thing through.

Murray phoned the next day. He said he felt sorry for me and he would return two days before Christmas so I wouldn't have to be alone. He added that he had called Alice to invite her to join us at his cabin for Christmas dinner. He also announced he would roast a turkey for the event. I spent Christmas Eve sitting on my treeless living room floor, listening to carols and other related selections. Julie and Cyndi had sent a box of little gifts, individually wrapped so as to drag out the tradition. I couldn't stop crying until Alice came up with an eggnog drink. And then Murray popped in to talk about the Christmas Day plan. The evening turned out to be better than anticipated, thanks to my two unlikely best friends.

However, once I crawled in bed, the night dragged on endlessly. The lonely feeling came back and I lay awake, feeling the same emptiness that I knew my daughters must be feeling a thousand miles away. I felt devastated and was reminded again of how I had never in my life been alone, totally dependent on myself. That reality shook me, and I was determined to face it head-on.

Charlotte Plantz

Just as I sank into a deep sleep, there was a loud knock on my door. It felt very early. Peering through glazed eyes I saw Murray standing in the doorway. He was positively glowing. "What do you want so early," I growled. "Merry Christmas. Ho, ho, ho," he shouted. Come with me. I want to show you something," he urged. Secretly I was delighted to see the ever-present-thorn-in-my-side. The thought of waking up to an empty house had been unbearable, but there was no time for that with Murray there.

"Do you want some coffee first?" I asked. "No, hurry, come on. Let's go. I'll bring you right back." The morning was crisp and clear. A few patches of snow remained from the last storm, and there were crystals floating in the freezing sunbeams, creating a Christmas-like feeling. It felt marvelous to be out in the early morning before people were moving around the roads. Murray headed his new Jeep, (that he had recently traded for his truck), up the narrow, winding road to the little canyon where he lived. The cabin was located in a beautiful, serene setting with wonderful smells all around.

Murray had always been full of surprising behavior so I didn't question him as he pulled into his driveway. When he opened the cabin door, I smelled the surprise before setting eyes on it. A perfectly shaped, large pine tree stood majestically in the middle of the cabin, still damp from the morning frost. The symbolism was more intense because the tree was unadorned.

"It's incredible," I shouted. "I can't believe it," choking on the words, as tears began to well up in my already burned-out eyes. The tears felt more like a flood of relief than any other emotion. My young friend looked at me and smiled as he said softly, "Merry Christmas, Charlotte."

Me and My Magical Life

No more words were needed, as my gift to Murray and Alice began to take form in my mind. "Quick, take me home, Murray. I have a lot to do." Words tumbled out as my mind raced ahead to an idea already in progress. He looked around the cluttered cabin, apparently realizing he too had a lot of work to do. We tore back down the mountain, calculating how long each of us needed for the day's preparations. As host, Murray was in charge of turkey and dressing. I had salad and pies, and Alice was in charge of vegetables and rolls. It was to be a feast at two o'clock.

Somewhere in my closet was a big bag of plastic baking crystals, which I set out to find. I ran downstairs to Alice for egg cartons, and didn't wait to be asked why. Back upstairs, I fairly flew around, packing a basket with treasures that would be my gift to Murray and Alice. At the appointed time, Alice and I met on her front porch, each of us laden with treats for the day's festivities.

By the time Murray picked us up he had already tucked the turkey into the oven. We walked into his cabin, heady with roasting bird and Christmas tree smells. The old woman's eyes were dancing with delight as I unpacked the basket filled with craft supplies. Murray set the turkey out, and I got busy with the crystals, pouring them into holiday shapes. They were baked in the hot oven for a few moments, causing them to blend together in crystal-clear forms. Candle wax was melted and poured into four, one-dozen egg cartons, lined with foil. Each egg holder contained a tiny piece of wick. My work was nearly finished.

Dinner was heavenly. We congratulated one another on culinary feats, helping ourselves to one last bite until we were unable to move. Murray suggested a walk, and Alice rose to join him. I stayed behind to put my gift together. Decorating Murray's gift tree restored my belief in the human spirit and filled me with joy. The clear plastic ornaments caught the light from the wood stove, transposing them into objects of creative fantasy.

By the time Murray and Alice returned, the tree was ready for the grand finale. We positioned ourselves around the stove, sinking back in soft overstuffed chairs. The only light came from the glow of the fire. I hopped up to light the candles as quickly as possible. One by one, the tiny lights began to transform the tree into a sparkling jewel, casting a soft glow about the room. The effect was breathtaking. When the last candle was lit, Murray began reading a poem by William Blake, carrying us off into yet another world.

I felt so much love for the old woman and young man that it became an ache, feeling vaguely familiar. Suddenly, I realized the ache was universal. It was the same one I felt for my daughters. The same ache felt by widows and widowers, sons going off to war, kids leaving home for college or lovers parting. It was the ache of loneliness and the need we all have for one another. The thought comforted me and made me feel stronger.

Just as we were about to slip into a state of melancholy, the tree caught fire. We leapt up simultaneously, running around the burning tree, laughing madly as we each dealt with the minor blaze. The tree was too green to be a serious threat. Minutes later, falling back into the comfort of the overstuffed chairs, exhausted by the day's excitement, yet glowing from the warmth of the experience, we were unable to exchange another word.

10
One-Way Ticket to Mexico

The idea to buy a one-way ticket to Mexico came about because of an American Indian art teacher who challenged me during an independent study class I had taken with him. Also because of a speech I had just written for speech class that was titled "Overcoming Bureaucratic Hyperbole." In the midst of my speech, I realized I was in the wrong school, or at least the wrong place at that exact time in my life. My faculty advisor, a wonderful art teacher named Elmer Schooley, had recently advised me to get serious about a major.

Because Highlands University had long specialized in turning out teachers, Schooley urged me toward a teaching degree in early education. But by then I knew for sure I did not want to spend the remainder of my life teaching children English, history, or math. I simply had to be an artist. My life seemed destined for that on every level. My advisor and the Indian art teacher just clarified it for me. My speech clinched it.

That day in the American Indian art teacher's office left no doubt in my mind about my next life choice. He described an art school in San Miguel de Allende, Mexico. He said he had gone there a few years earlier for a master's degree in art. And then he said, "The Instituto is where you should be, not here in New Mexico, pursuing an education degree." The man tossed a catalog from the Instituto Allende to me, and it fell short of my grasp and landed on the floor. As I bent to pick it up, the pages opened to the centerfold, where a picture of an interior courtyard showed students involved in a crafts fair. I swear my blood began to flow to a Latin beat. I knew that I would attend that school, no matter what.

That night, I dreamed I was dancing on a tabletop in a Mexican cantina with people all around me clapping to the music and cheering me on. The next day I went to the registrar's office and withdrew from school. My colleagues overreacted, because by then I was eligible for a scholastic grant that would help pay for my tuition. With financial aid, I was ensured completion of my education. It was the end of February, with just a few more weeks to the end of the quarter, but I knew I could wait no longer. I had to withdraw right then.

Murray was thrilled and confused by my decision. He was thrilled by my audacity but devastated when I told him it would be a solo experience. Murray had been excited about a photography course he read about in the Instituto Allende catalog and assumed that he would accompany me on such a great adventure. From that day, our friendship took on a completely different tone.

Murray began to follow me around campus, several paces behind me, dressed in a long tweed overcoat that was two sizes too big for his thin body. He dragged one leg, limping like a wounded animal, imploring me to let him join me. When people asked him what was wrong, he said he was practicing to beg for pesos on the streets in Mexico. I did laugh at the absurdity of his actions, but then realized he was serious about wanting to go, so I tried not to tease him.

Me and My Magical Life

Little did I know how serious he was, but by then I was so caught up in my own sense of adventure that I thought of nothing except how to get there, because I had virtually no money. I had been living on work-study wages, a pittance with no reserve resources whatsoever. However, I did have magic. Once again it came through for me, in the form of a letter from my ex-husband: he informed me that he had just sold a three-acre piece of land that we owned. Enclosed was a check for twenty-five hundred dollars.

Another stroke of luck came as a request by Barry and Cathy. They had decided to take a trip to California. They asked whether I would like to stay at their place in Chacon until I could get my life together for my next venture. They were going to drive their pickup truck and were happy to take most of my belongings back to California. Everything came together so quickly I hardly had time to think about the reality of my decision. And a good thing too, for what I was undertaking felt daunting. Not to mention, my total inexperience at traveling or living in a foreign country, especially because I didn't speak the language or know anyone in that country.

What I needed just then was a dose of faith, so I invited my nun friend, Joanna, to accompany me to Chacon for the weekend. Neither of us had a car, so Murray agreed to drive us. He promised to come back for Joanna early Sunday evening because they still had classes. I would stay on for the rest of the week to ponder my sanity in making such a rash decision. In my purse I had the airline ticket for California, where I would spend two months with my daughters and apply to the Instituto Allende. My plan had been set in motion and there was nothing left to do but continue moving forward.

Charlotte Plantz

The thought of spending a week alone in the Sangre de Cristo Mountains, with a ghost village nearly in my backyard, during the month of March, now makes me shudder. However, at the time, it seemed like a great idea. Chacon has always had a reputation as one of the coldest places in the state and was referred to as Little Alaska by locals. The solitude was like a welcome stranger. My life had been filled with too many people needing shelter, and there was nothing more I could do for them.

And so I turned inward, to Herman Hesse, Goethe, and Thomas Hardy, and they sustained me throughout my isolation. On a moonless night, I sat in the outhouse listening to a pack of coyotes, unusually close to the house. They were howling at the top of their lungs. A wave of euphoria swept over me as I realized how comfortable I felt sitting there by myself, miles from human beings, being serenaded by a pack of wild animals. The next morning I awoke to a foot of snow on the ground. The coyotes must have been celebrating the approaching storm, and I felt privileged being witness to that.

I prayed I could keep fires going, and thanks to Mike Plantz there was ample chopped firewood still left from his summer efforts. However, if a huge blizzard dumped a couple feet of snow, there was no way in or out except by horseback. Pedro Abeyta probably would have loved the idea of rescuing me.

Bessie had told me a story about living in the same house during the late fifties with six little children when such a storm did come along, marooning them for days. She became so desperate to get out of the house she talked her husband into hooking up a team of horses to the old blue Ford. Away they went, the car filled with laughing children and their parents being pulled down the mountainside to church by Pedro's faithful team.

Me and My Magical Life

Cathy and Barry experienced a similar storm in the spring of 1973, when Barry was teaching school in Taos and couldn't get home for several days. When he finally made it back to Chacon, the National Guard had arrived with food for the people, and some of it was being delivered by tank. Cathy stood on her porch in the blinding sun, surrounded by feet of snow, listening to unfamiliar sounds coming toward her. Soon she saw a huge, dark object crawling slowly up the mountain. Sitting on top of the lumbering tank, waving wildly was her husband. He was holding a big carton of groceries, and grinning as an airplane flew low overhead, dropping bales of hay onto the fields below.

I had no wish for such an adventure. Bringing the nun along gave me hope for my faith in prayer and the weather, among other things. Joanna was also a great cookstove tender. She enjoyed the simple act of sitting in front of the old Majestic relic, prayerfully feeding small pieces of wood into the fiery chamber. Her reward would later be a blueberry pie that had baked for a couple of hours at a low temperature and high altitude.

Nuns make great friends if you need a lot of quiet time and solitude. Since Joanna was completely content with her task, I took the opportunity to climb up the mountain above the house so I could sit and contemplate the uncertainty of what lay ahead of me. I had a multitude of questions that I threw out to the wind, aloud. I questioned my relationship with my daughters, and what I was doing to them. I questioned the force that seemed to be driving me toward so many unknowns. I questioned my reasons for wanting to venture so far out on the edge of life. I was forsaking family, old friends, and especially, a way of life that was no longer tolerable. What was the source of the incredible need I had to live a simple, creative life? Most of all, I questioned my sanity, but each time I threw out a question, the wind seemed to blow an answer back into my consciousness.

By the time my rear end was growing numb from sitting on a cold rock, I felt most of my questions had been answered, and some of my greatest fears laid to rest, at least for the time being. I strolled back down to the house, feeling something akin to euphoria. Or it could have been the altitude, or the smell of piñon smoke curling up out of the ancient stovepipe, reminding me of the blueberry pie that I could smell as I approached the cluttered front porch.

Joanna was still sitting in front of the stove, looking saintly in her black robe and white wimple, smiling blissfully as I entered. She asked whether I had found the answers to my questions. Words began to pour out of my mouth, as though in a flood of relief. I was so happy to have a friend with the patience to hear me out without interruption.

As I finally ran out of words, Joanna looked down at the smooth, worn wooden floor and then slowly up at me again before speaking. Her voice was soft and thoughtful. "This is the story of my life. Here I am, the holy woman, and all I can think about is the blueberry pie in the oven, while you go out and throw questions to the wind, and come back with all the answers."

Our eyes met and held as we each pondered her response, and then we both burst out laughing, until it seemed we would never stop. We laughed until we cried: a short, plump holy woman, and a tall, thin wild woman, baking a blueberry pie on the side of a mountain, in the middle of nowhere. During the height of winter, with no way out, taking directions from the wind!

Me and My Magical Life

Murray came for Joanna as planned, leaving me to fend for myself while the two of them continued with school. We had agreed Murray would stay in the apartment until my departure. The rent was paid until the end of the month, and it would save him the daily drive from Gallinas Canyon into Las Vegas. No easy commute during winter. I still had to tell Alice I would be leaving, something I did not look forward to because of her fantasy of my remaining in Las Vegas and being a part of her crafts store operation.

When I returned to town and broke the news to my dear landlady, all hell broke loose. Alice went completely berserk, even going so far as to enter my apartment and remove a brand-new stereo I had saved for. The neighbors across the hall had seen her carrying the stereo out of my place, so I confronted her and asked the reason for her act. She screamed at me, calling me a traitor and ranting about my indifference to her. She was beyond hysterical, and I was really quite concerned for her health. I phoned her daughter in Mora and asked for her advice in calming her mother, but the daughter said Alice had a tendency toward such behavior when things didn't go her way. It was not how I wanted to leave an otherwise wonderful friend and experience.

To make matters worse, Alice wouldn't give me my stereo, and I was forced to have a policeman get it for me. I had asked Murray to come give me moral support when the policeman confronted Alice. As the machine was handed over to me, Alice picked up a broom and began beating Murray with it. The young officer, trying not to laugh, stepped forward and removed the broom from Alice's hand, while trying to calm her with soft words. He turned to me and said, "Geez, she's a little old woman. That was a shock." I tried one more time to see Alice before I left Las Vegas, but she wouldn't open her door to me. It was a very sad way to leave the intimate social life we had created together.

Murray drove me to Albuquerque to board a plane for Sacramento and the reunion with my daughters. In spite of Murray's nonstop badgering to be included in my plan, my focus was entirely on the upcoming trip. I couldn't stop thinking about heading toward an art-filled life as a single woman. When nothing else worked for Murray, he began his old tirade about how I would probably meet some horrible fate. Like dying of thirst in the desert or being carried off by bandits or something worse. By the time we got to the ticket counter, my young friend seemed to realize that we were about to go our separate ways.

Suddenly, we both felt the pain of separation. We had, after all, been through a lot together, not to mention he had come to my rescue in California when I needed a ride out of the state toward a new life. On some strange level, Murray and I had become a team, each of us struggling to find a creative solution to our own survival. We had been a source of strength and courage for each other during some pretty trying situations, and from that point on, we would have to find our own separate ways. Murray never cried, but that didn't stop me. I cried halfway to Sacramento from relief, sadness, and joy.

Julie and Cyndi picked me up at the airport and immediately entered into my delirious state of possibilities for the future, even though it meant they would be without their mother for another block of time, a time of vital importance to their own human development. Because I had been well trained from birth not to form strong bonds with other people, including my own children, sisters, brother, grandparents, aunts,

Me and My Magical Life

uncles, and particularly friends, I was naive enough to believe that I could walk away from all of them and not leave any negative marks whatsoever.

But, I had to do something that would change the direction for my daughters and myself, so we could be cut free from the endless circle of negative extended family behavior. I had heard myself sound like my mother on enough occasions to feel alarmed. The thought of becoming her had me concerned. And I still believed that their father was a loving, caring, and just human being, who could provide them the stability they needed for a while longer. Beyond all that, I had become a driven woman, one who could not be stopped from finding a different life for myself.

The girls' father was gracious in moving out of the house for the next two and a half months while I prepared for the Mexico adventure. It would take time getting a visa and applying to the Instituto Allende, and then waiting for their acceptance or rejection. Meanwhile, life with my daughters fell easily back into place. I cooked, cleaned, and baked cookies to have on the old worn oak table when the girls came home from school. Just as before I went away, we sat with their friends around the table in the middle of the kitchen and talked for an hour or two about everything imaginable, something we had been doing for years.

And then another development came up that I had not anticipated and set in motion a whole new set of problems to be worked out. A letter came from Mike Plantz, who was then living in Eureka, California. He worked the night shift as a green chain puller at Simpson Timber lumber mill. Pulling green chain is a brutal job; men work outdoors beneath a roof, usually in the rain, pulling up to twenty-foot lengths of wet

Charlotte Plantz

redwood lumber off a moving chain and stacking them on a dolly. A pair of leather gloves had to be replaced each week. Mike had lived and worked in the same place before he set out for New Mexico that previous summer. He had gone through his thousand-dollar savings and returned to his former job.

Nearly seven months later, there I was, sitting in my old kitchen, reading a letter from Mike. He invited me to visit him in Humboldt County because he had so many beautiful places he wanted to show me before I headed south. Mike was living with his sister, Sue, her husband, Dale, and their three young children, Davy, Jennie, and Becky. He assured me his family would be delighted to have me as their guest. It was an intriguing thought. Mike and I had become good friends, and found we had many things in common, in particular the great outdoors. I had never been to Humboldt County, with its redwood forests and pounding surf, so I was instantly taken by the idea. I loved the ocean, especially the wild parts, and I knew that section of coastline was known for its wildness.

There was just one problem: I had to be very careful with the money I had just received from the land sale, and I did not own a car. Eureka is three hundred miles from Folsom, and not an easy place to get to unless you go by automobile, so I reluctantly gave up on the idea. The next morning I was hanging laundry, pondering Mike's invitation, when I threw the problem to the wind, which just happened to be blowing. My question was simply put: if I was supposed to visit Mike, some things would have to happen to make it possible.

And then it seemed like I moved into slow motion. I can still see myself, hanging sheets and towels. Driving ever so slowly into the picture, the mail truck appeared. It stopped at our box on the road, and I stood

90

for a while, as though in a trance, until a gust of wind shook me out of my reverie. I hung the last of the laundry and headed down the driveway to fetch the mail.

To my amazement, there were envelopes from art galleries, something from out of my past that I had forgotten about. I sat on the front steps, tearing open each envelope as though something might jump out at me. And things did; checks jumped out, one after another. I could hardly believe my eyes. I did a rough total of around seven hundred dollars. With my mouth still agape, I ran in to answer the phone that was ringing.

It was my brother, the car salesman, phoning to tell me he had found a great used Toyota that I could have for four hundred dollars. I asked how soon I could pick up the car, and he said to come the next day. For me, it was the "sign" I needed. It was magic all right! I picked up the phone and dialed Mike's sister's number, knowing he worked swing shift and might be at home. He was there, and it was wonderful hearing his voice after so many months.

We set a date for my visit that would take place a week and a half later. Mike was thrilled I would be coming, and I was thrilled to be going, for we both knew it was pleasant spending time together. Mike and I could talk about anything, and I needed to talk about men, and why I couldn't seem to comprehend "dating" or "signals." If a man was trying to make a pass, I missed it completely. My daughters had teased me about that every time I went home. Mike was the perfect person to help prepare me for my great adventure as a single woman in a Latin country.

The girls' father was being extremely generous in trying to accommodate my needs. I think that had a lot to do with relief at being able to live his life of honky-tonk bars and women openly. For eighteen years he had played the role of suburban gentleman, husband, and father, all while living quite a different life after hours. When I told Fabian that I wanted to take a trip north, he assured me that it wasn't an inconvenience. He would move back into the house until I returned. My ex-husband did, however, make one request.

He asked that I meet him at a bar called Cow Town so I could meet his new girlfriend, Jeannie. It seemed like a reasonable request under the circumstances, so that Friday night I drove into the Cow Town parking lot with a nervous chuckle. Bars were so far from my personal reality, just walking through the door, a lone woman, took all the courage I could muster. Fabian knew that, but that was his world, and I knew he wanted me to see him in it, so in I went.

The shock was palpable. It reminded me of the bar scene in the first Star Wars movie: full of alien characters. The place was filled with women in bleached, beehive hairdos, miniskirts, pancake makeup-and cigarettes held to bright red mouths. Men with slicked-down hair, smelling of pungent aftershave lotion, were swaying slightly to the honky-tonk music that filtered from the dark recess at the back of the bar.

I stood alone in the gloomy neon light, hair straight to my shoulders, dressed in a green sweater, pleated plaid skirt, and green tights that looked even more garish under the fluorescent light. I felt like a freak, given the setting, and realized that all eyes were on me as Fabian stepped forward to greet me. He turned toward the crowd and stated, "This is my ex-wife."

There was a collective drawing in of breath and a few nervous laughs, and then a few people spoke to me, welcoming me to their world. I did hear someone say, "Who would have believed," as I headed toward the bar stool being offered me. Jeannie seemed like a nice woman, and after a drink, Fabian suggested we go to another of his favorite haunts to dance.

My first thought was, "Oh boy!" but something pushed me on. I realized it was important to the man to whom I had been married for many years to establish his true identity in front of all his friends, with his ex-wife present. It was a rite of passage for us both. The next bar was really a dance hall, with a large band belting out country and western tunes. Poor Fabian, all those years with me, having to endure classical and international music, and heaven forbid-New Age music. No wonder he fled to another world. I must admit that by then I was curious about his world and the people who inhabited it. The three of us sat at the bar and ordered drinks. Shortly, a man approached and asked me to dance. I excused myself to join him, as Fabian whispered, "That's a married man you are about to dance with." The irony did not escape me. I danced with a couple of other men and then the band took a break.

A younger band member came over and asked what someone like me was doing in a place like that. I laughed, and introduced him to my ex-husband and Jeannie. Turned out, Jeff was the lead guitar player, who couldn't help but wonder what my story was. He asked if I would step outside with him so we could talk, and he could get some fresh air and smoke a cigarette. Fabian had been watching, as I turned to him and asked if he would watch my purse while I stepped outside with the guitar player.

It was a strange moment, and not lost on the musician. Jeff turned out to be someone I could actually relate to in that foreign place. At the end of the second set, the guitar player asked if we could meet again, on another day, in a different setting. I explained that I was just about to leave for a trip north to visit an old friend. From there, I would soon be leaving Folsom, on a one-way ticket to Mexico. The guitar player said, "Too bad. Well, if it doesn't work out here's my phone number. I would like to see you again and hear your story."

11
Visit to Humboldt County

After I picked up the little blue Toyota from my brother, dealt with the title change, and danced the night away at The Hitching Post, I was ready to head for a visit with Mike. I couldn't believe that I would drive six hours for a chat, but the man was so easy to talk to. I was desperate to talk about my wild idea of studying art in Mexico, and who better to share that with than my new best friend. It had been nearly seven months since I had driven a car, so the physical act was quite heady. For a while I drove with the window down so I could feel the wind on my face. I needed to feel that I was truly alive, and most of all, free to explore all the back roads of life.

I had studied a map and carefully plotted my route on a winding two-lane road through the Lake Country that would connect with Highway 101 above Ukiah. Soon I was pretty much alone, cruising through lovely hill country. Window open, my face blasted by cold air and singing loudly, the world held nothing but promise for me. Though the Toyota did sound a bit loud with the window down. I just sang louder.

I drove the three hundred miles in awe, at times bursting into tears at the sheer beauty of the land. The closer I drew to my destination, the more beautiful it became. I was about to enter a world of redwood forests and ferns and wild rivers. You do not see the Pacific Ocean from the highway until after you pass through Eureka, but by then that is icing on the cake of landscapes with even more to come. Humboldt County may be one of the most beautiful places on earth, and you have to be plenty hardy to endure the continuously cold, damp, foggy weather, not to mention floods, mudslides, earthquakes, and wild winter storms that topple hundred-foot trees. It is not a place for the faint of heart.

Toward the last leg of my journey I began to think about Mike Plantz and our friendship. He was the most open, honest person I had ever met. Besides his prowess with an axe, he was acutely aware of nature and his place within it. His photography was a tribute to that aspect of life as he saw it. The man captured it beautifully and was able to express the same sentiments in his writing and verbal thoughts.

I had watched Mike during that summer go off on long walks alone with his camera, just for the pleasure of capturing some little miracle of life. He used to wear a big military jacket that had a dozen pockets. Over time, I watched as he pulled out a flower or dried pod, sometimes raisins or nuts, and once on a backpacking trip, a little bottle of honey mead wine.

When I met Mike, he had a full beard and was wearing that oversized jacket that made him look like a giant. I remember being stunned when we met again and I realized he was not much taller than me and weighed not more than thirty pounds over my weight. His feet, however, were huge, something we have always laughed about. Mike had sent good directions to his sister's place, so I had no trouble finding it. He said he heard me coming long before he saw the car. Being such an observant soul, as I exited the car, Mike reached in and shut down the choke. He was laughing at how I had not noticed the loud revving sound.

Mike was between jobs so had plenty of time to show me his favorite haunts. His sister and family were delighted to have me as their guest. As I entered the house, the three little children were lined up on the couch smiling shyly. They looked like little storybook dolls. I did not believe I had ever seen such adorable children. They were all of diminutive size and close in age. Becky, the youngest, was not quite one year old. Davy and Jennie looked like their mom and dad in miniature.

As Mike helped carry my things into his room, I noticed a round waterbed in the middle of his bedroom. He was carrying my sleeping bag and said we would bring cushions from the couch for me, since his bed would sleep only one comfortably. As I continued to discover about Mike, everything for him was matter of fact. There were never hidden meanings or innuendos and certainly never sexual connotations of any kind. That just was not him.

I knew in that instant that this man would be the best friend I would ever have. We had already shared a room at Barry and Cathy's, so I was perfectly comfortable with the physical closeness that his small bedroom demanded. I actually loved it when we crawled into our respective beds that night after a lovely evening with his family. We lay in the dark and talked for a long time, catching up on the months since Mike's departure from New Mexico and all the exciting things he wanted to share with me while I was there. Mike and I had always been good sleepers so we awoke full of energy and ready to greet the new day.

The next few days were filled with beauty and adventure as we explored every special nook and cranny of Mike's world. Because we were both poor, we packed lunches and found ourselves eating in the most divine places imaginable: one time in the rain beneath umbrellas as we perched on a rocky outcropping where crashing surf blew spray up over us. Another time we were on the beach at College Cove, sitting near a waterfall that cascaded down and across the beach, where a blowhole on a tiny island with redwood trees sent plumes of water high into the misty air right in front of our eyes. The beach was strewn with massive redwood logs that had been rolling around at high tide for eons. Sometimes they would pile up like giant pick-up sticks until the next high tide rolled in.

At some point on that beach Mike and I were lying on our stomachs in the warm sand, watching tiny sand crabs scurry about as waves moved slowly in and out. We decided that we wanted to be nothing more than sand and water. I became sand because I have always been a trifle terrified of water, and Mike became water, for the opposite reason. Mike shared with his mother and sister the most amazing ability to float in water for hours if need be, completely relaxed and at peace with the world. Put me in water over my head and I would flail myself to death.

As Mike and I lay there being sand and water, I believe we both felt the first stirrings of what that symbolized. Whatever it was, it felt quite wonderful. Nothing else changed. The two of us just kept exploring beautiful places and enjoying one another's company. We slogged through muddy trails at Redwood State Park so Mike could show me the first, third, and fifth tallest redwood trees in the world. It was an extraordinary sight and it was then we dubbed Humboldt County "Little Sky Country." That phrase became a great source of humor

Me and My Magical Life

between us. Years later we chose to live in a place that had the exact opposite quality, with the joke still fresh in our minds.

In the same park we traversed a slick, muddy trail through the forest and found ourselves on Gold Beach. Suddenly, we had to scurry back into the trees as a huge herd of Roosevelt elk thundered down the beach, some of them kicking up spray from the shallow water that was being washed in by the tide. That had to be one of our most memorable moments together. We both trembled with fear and delight as our hearts pounded wildly.

In some primitive way, the experience was slightly erotic, and we moved slightly apart, taking care not to brush up against each other. By then a heightened sense of awareness had already awakened, and the air between us felt more charged. On we explored: Big Lagoon, Dry Lagoon, and a few others whose names I no longer recall, but there is nothing quite like a North Coast lagoon, some separated by a thin sand bar just out of the clutch of the pounding surf. Some of the lagoons are covered with masses of water lilies: a Monet painting when in bloom.

Big Lagoon was a small community of tiny cottages built in the twenties or thirties. It had always served as a vacation getaway, with all the cottages built around a large, lush green common park. The miniature dwellings were covered with green moss that gave the place the look of a fairyland where you expected gnomes to come tumbling out through all the doors. The entire setting was surrounded on three sides by redwood forests.

The massive trees created a very small sky and as a result, hazy sunbeams became filtered by all the branches so that the whole place was bathed in an eerie ghostly haze that never ceased to thrill us. To the west the constant roar of surf reminded us how precarious those little buildings were, some of them perched on the edge of a small cliff. Actually, several houses plunged into the ocean a few years later when the North Coast experienced some huge storms.

Mike and I had offered to babysit the children that particular evening so Sue and Dale could get out for some well-earned R & R. We sent them on their way and prepared the evening meal for our charges. We got them bathed and read to and finally popped into bed. They were extremely mellow children and did their parents proud. Mike and I had our dinner with candlelight and soft music. We spent the evening going over our day in minute detail, not wanting it to end. By then we were acutely aware of the charged air between us. Mike went to shower while I cleaned up the kitchen.

When he finished it was my turn, and as I entered the warm, steamy room I could detect a slight odor of the man who had just left and my knees went limp. We met later on the living room couch in front of a television that neither of us was interested in but was powerless to turn off. I think we needed the diversion, for we kept scooting farther and farther apart.

Perhaps it was all those charged ions along the beach actually pushing us away from each other. Whatever it was, it made us both edgy and slightly jumpy. When I could no longer stand the tension, I jumped up and turned the television off. Turning, I faced Mike and asked what was going on between us. He was good at hiding his feelings so I was surprised when he blurted out, "I feel like you need to go to Mexico and find yourself, and I don't want to stand in your way. But if I touch you, I couldn't bear to let go of you." It took a while for that to sink in as my mind flew around the room trying to find a safe place to land.

Me and My Magical Life

I finally spoke, saying it was time for me to go back home to Folsom. I would leave the next day. At least that broke some of the tension. Mike asked me to go with him to Arcata Redwood Park the next morning for one last excursion. Neither of us slept very well that night in our separate beds. We could each hear the other tossing and turning and were both glad for morning.

Arcata Redwood Park sits in the middle of the little town of Arcata, home to Humboldt State University, located on the other side of the park. Mike and I were quick to notice the small sky in the park, with that ever-present filtered light coming down as beams through the tall trees. Predictably, it cast a spell over the place and sounds seemed hushed, perhaps simply soaked up by all the moisture. The ground beneath the trees was covered with ferns and masses of delicate white trilliums. It was another fairyland that slightly tricked your senses.

Mike and I rode the merry-go-round, taking turns pushing each other around and around until we got too dizzy to go on with it. Finally we were on the swings, pushing ourselves higher and higher by our fierce pumping of knees and legs. Mike had been telling me about Hawaii and how he would love to share that place with me. He said perhaps when I returned from my Mexico experience the two of us could go live for a while among the pineapples on one of the Hawaiian Islands. I told him I thought we could do that. And then it was time for me to get on the road.

By then, with talk of living together yet not being able to make physical contact, I personally was a nervous wreck. I did say that I was terrified by the thought of buying a one-way ticket to Mexico. Especially when I didn't know a soul in that country, or speak the language. Mike thought about that for a moment and then responded in a serious tone, "If you do go to Mexico, you might regret it for a while. But if you don't go, you may regret it for the rest of your life." That was all I needed to hear and my blood began to pulse to that Latin beat again. We hugged and felt ourselves hesitate when it was time to let go. It did seem to go on for a long time and then Mike kissed me on the cheek as I blinked back tears.

We drove to the little Toyota that was packed and ready to roll, and Mike teased me about the choke, saying, "You should get better gas mileage this time." Since neither of us could bear the suspense, I quickly jumped in the car, put it in gear, and started off toward the next phase of my life. Twenty miles down the highway I began to cry, then sob to the point where I had to pull off to the side. It took all my effort to keep from turning around and flying back to Mike and his kindness and wisdom and sense of fun and joy of life on the simplest terms. Finally, I was able to get myself under control and proceed with my life's journey.

I arrived back in Folsom around nine p.m. and the girls were still up. I had phoned earlier, telling them when I would return. Their father had slipped back into his other life, now a shadow in mine. I told Julie and Cyndi all the details of my trip. Since they had known Mike that previous summer, they would have a deeper understanding of the personal relationship parts of the story.

My daughters have always been highly sensitive and open to all people, and I appreciated their insight and input. The girls liked Mike a lot and thought him to be an exceptionally nice man. We had a few good chuckles over male/female signals in trying to relate. After the girls retired I was too wired to sleep, so I sat down at the old kitchen table, pen in hand, and began to write a letter to Mike.

Me and My Magical Life

By the time my hand became numb, I was stunned to realize I had written twelve pages! I thanked Mike for showing me such an incredible time and then launched into a prolonged discourse on the jumpy state of behavior between us. I ended the letter with something to the effect that I was terrified when it came to relating to the opposite sex once it moved outside the realm of a brother/sister relationship. I added that I had strong feelings for him and had wanted to crawl into that too-small round waterbed with him and never get out. I ended with something like: "Now that you know how weird I really am, I'll probably never see you again. Goodbye forever, your friend Charlotte."

I folded the thick confessional and stuffed it in an envelope, sealed it with a stamp, and mailed it the next morning. I felt such relief that I was able to go to bed and sleep like a log late into the day. Within the week I had a ten-page letter from Mike that ended with: "Far out, I felt the same way but did not want to alter your plans for Mexico. When you return, we'll take up from where we left off and see what happens." What a friend! Mike gave me the courage to go on with my life. And I knew that he would be there waiting for me when I returned.

12
Mexico, Here I Come

A whirlwind of activity took up the next few weeks. Then it was time to buy that ambiguous one-way ticket and board a plane for Mexico City. Had it not been for the enthusiasm of my daughters, I would have walked away from the opportunity I had set up for myself. I still find it difficult to believe that they could be so supportive, given the circumstances. However, Julie and Cyndi were the ones to literally push me through the runway gate toward my fate. I had transferred the Toyota to Julie's name and handed her the keys as we left the house for the airport. I was much too nervous to drive that day and so grateful for my daughter's good driving skills.

I had chosen a white cotton dress to wear and it had a row of fabric-covered buttons that closed the entire front of the dress. When it came time for me to pass through the runway gate, one of the buttons broke loose and began rolling across the tarmac. As I stooped to retrieve the button, I turned back toward the terminal, and my daughters, but they were waving and shouting at me to get on the plane and go be an artist. Once again, something propelled me toward the waiting plane. In a complete state of shock, I boarded and settled in for the ride of my life.

Charlotte Plantz

It took a while to realize that in some bizarre way, I had created such an atmosphere of positive enthusiasm that my daughters were caught up in the excitement of facing their own adventures. Even though it meant they would be without their mother for six months. Cyndi and I had gone to the river the day before, walking the trails and finally sitting on a bridge that spanned a small creek that wound its way through the park to the river. Cyndi took a piece of paper out of her pocket. As she unfolded it, she looked at me, saying she thought I would be surprised by what she had written.

Cyndi had written a poem about our life together. She understood what I needed to do at that time. My amazing daughter, at fourteen, was able to comprehend what was unfolding. I was flabbergasted because the child had never shown an interest in poetry, but more so by the content. It was a beautiful poem and I was deeply touched by her keen insight. We both cried for the beauty and pain of life. The two of us emerged from that densely shaded forest into dazzling sunlight, aware that something wonderful had just passed between us.

The Aero Mexicano plane left Los Angeles, where I had changed from a domestic flight out of Sacramento. The moment I stepped onto that plane I knew Mexico was the destination for me. The plane was filled with Spanish-speaking people, and I thrilled at the soft, lyrical sounds rippling up and down the aisles. My high school Spanish was by then so far back in my memory bank not one word was decipherable. However, that did not frighten me in the least, it just made me more anxious to learn the language. I had been sure to include a Spanish class in my choice of classes at the Instituto.

When the plane landed in Mexico City, there was no time for reflection. I grabbed a taxi and held on for dear life as the driver tore through jammed streets to the bus station. From there I boarded a first class bus for the one hundred fifty miles to San Miguel de Allende. The bus arrived in late afternoon at the picturesque little city that has been a National Treasure for many years. There was no station. The bus merely stopped on a narrow cobblestone street a few blocks from the main plaza.

The assistant driver opened the luggage compartment on the side of the bus and set my bags in front of me on the narrow sidewalk. At that moment, the reality of what I had chosen hit me hard. Not one person around me was speaking English. My head began to buzz and my vision blurred. As the bus pulled off in a cloud of exhaust fumes, I had to fight to keep from fainting. I stepped into a recessed doorway, tears pouring as I fought to maintain composure.

Finally, I was able to blow my nose, dry my eyes, and approach someone with the name of the hotel where I had a reservation written on a piece of paper. I was also able to say in halting Spanish that I did not speak the language. The man smiled and led me to a corner, where he pointed down the street to a sign with the hotel name on it. Gathering my wits and bags, neither of which was very easy, I trundled down the uneven walkway in my white cotton dress with its missing button.

As I approached the lovely old hotel, I noticed perspiration rings around my armpits and sweat trickling down my back. When I entered the hotel I was surrounded by beautiful Mexican tiles and huge rooms that opened onto a courtyard with a big fountain in the center. However, I thought I would die on the spot from an immediate sense of loneliness. I fell on the bed in my room and sobbed until I sensed the day was coming to an end.

Charlotte Plantz

In the gloom of twilight, my predicament seemed even more daunting. What could I possibly have been thinking? Perhaps a shower would cheer me up, or at least make me smell better. I stood beneath the delicious hot water until my skin began to pucker, and that sent a message to my addled brain. I became aware of food smells and felt ravenous. I dressed and tentatively opened the door and stepped into the courtyard. It was May, one of the hottest months of the year in San Miguel de Allende, but at seven thousand feet elevation evenings were nothing short of glorious.

It felt as though I had woken from a deep sleep. The sound of water spilling from the fountain finally reached my consciousness, and the pungent aroma of flowers filled my nostrils. I stood for a long time, taking in sounds from the street just the other side of the high wall that enclosed the courtyard. I became aware of other smells that were completely foreign to me. All those voices sounded like a cacophony.

That fact alone nearly sent me back inside my lonely room. Once again, for the umpteenth time another force took over, propelling me out into the cobblestone street and the mass of people moving about. I found my way to the *Jardin* at the heart of the little city, and from that point on life would become bearable, for there were Americans. And they spoke my language.

The *Jardin*, which means garden in Spanish, was in reality a plaza with a gazebo in the center. A band was playing, something that was done every evening during warm weather. A sidewalk surrounded the *Jardin*, with shorter walkways radiating out from the gazebo like spokes in a wheel. Cast iron benches sat every few feet at the edges of the walkways. The plaza was filled with people of every age and stratum of life. The most amazing spectacle was the *caminita*, taking place on the outer walk: girls were walking in one direction on the inside, nearest the gazebo, while boys walked in the opposite direction on the outer edge.

I found an empty space on a bench and sat down to watch the procession. It was one of the few ways young people could interact in a place where cars hardly existed and strict social mores prevented teenagers from being together without a chaperone. I had forgotten about food, and all of a sudden my stomach began to growl audibly. Two Americans had joined me on the bench, and as we chatted they heard my hunger rumblings and suggested we adjourn to a restaurant across the street from the Jardin, where we could continue our conversation and satisfy hunger pangs at the same time.

The two Americans happened to be male, and as I continued to find over the next year, one's sexual identity had nothing to do with becoming friends. Those two became good pals until they returned to the states months later. Jimmy was a merchant marine based in New Orleans. A small and wiry man in his mid thirties with a soft southern accent, he loved to talk. He sort of reminded me of the singer Jimmy Buffet. Jimmy would ship out of New Orleans for a few months at a time on greasy, grimy oil tankers. The minute the ship returned to port he jumped on a plane and headed for San Miguel de Allende and a different life all together.

The other man, John, was from Texas. He was an oil well rigger between jobs, in Mexico for an extended vacation. John was about the same age and size as Jimmy, and his Texas drawl was even more drawn out. John had a wicked sense of humor, and that is what the three of us shared from that first dinner together. Between us, we had an immense capacity for finding humor in just about everything. I could not have been more fortunate to share a bench in the *Jardin* with those two southern oilmen, who sustained me with laughter through the next few months.

It was a great relief to awaken the next morning knowing the day was already organized for me. It was my first day to explore the Instituto, beginning with enrollment as a full time degree-seeking student. I was greeted in the office with the first shock of the day: my tuition check from California had not arrived. In fact, the check never arrived, but that turned out to work in my favor in the long run.

The office staff assured me that lost mail was simply a part of living in Mexico and I should not worry. I had arrived early to give myself a couple of weeks to get oriented with the country and culture, so I was at the school the week before spring quarter ended.

That was a good move on my part because I had the opportunity to sit in on classes and get a feel for what lay ahead. It also put me in the midst of a school bustling with activity rather than an empty environment. That surely would have daunted my enthusiasm, for by then I was ready to throw myself into a frenzy of busy work. I sat in the little coffee shop, filling out papers and listening in on conversations that seemed entirely in English.

That surprised me, and I later learned that almost everyone at the Instituto spoke English. In fact, nearly every student was either American, Canadian, or European. Learning Spanish proved to be difficult simply because I wasn't immersed in it as I had expected. My Spanish classes turned out to be invaluable, and for three years I never missed an opportunity to join my classmates sitting around a table in the shade on one of the many patios on campus.

Me and My Magical Life

Before I left the hotel that morning I had written Mike a twelve-page letter, regaling him with descriptions of my new world. But I also wrote of my loneliness and guilt at leaving my daughters, and my anxiety about being alone in a foreign country. The pages were filled with doubt and I ended the letter by saying, "I may have made a mistake." Because of the Mexican mail system, it took two weeks to get a reply from Mike. I was stunned to finally receive a postcard with big block letters that read: TRY HARDER! After the shock, and reminder of the woodpile incident the summer before, I propped the card on the nightstand and for months it gave me courage to keep going.

The next major project was to find housing. I scanned the bulletin board on a wall outside the coffee shop, hoping to find other students who were looking for housemates. Just as I had hoped, there were several opportunities. All I had to do was leave my name and a contact source, and before the day was out I would have a home. The first place was pretty far out in a *barrio*, which meant a long walk to school. However, I felt so lonely and desperate to get out of the hotel and among people that I put aside better judgment and accepted the first offer from two young women.

The house was crawling with mice, and one of the women had a cat that she loved watching as it pounced on mice and torment them before devouring the poor creatures. After about three evenings of cat and mouse, I found another house in the center of town just a few blocks from the Instituto, a real bonus during the fierce heat of May and June.

Two young women not much older than my seventeen year old daughter Julie, were full of fun and easy to be with in a much more enjoyable setting than my previous experience. Those two got me through infected ear lobes, the result of piercings my family doctor friend had insisted on as a going-away present.

The house itself was fun in that all the rooms opened onto a long, narrow courtyard open to the sky. The kitchen was divided into two sections: one room with sink, dish cupboards, and a worktable. The other room, across the courtyard, held the stove and refrigerator. The dining room and living room were two separate spaces at the end of the courtyard, so you were constantly indoors and out as you moved throughout the house. That was exciting when the summer monsoon arrived, with lightning striking all around and torrential rain coming down so fast the courtyard drains could not handle the volume. In those instances you had to scurry to move things out of the fast-rising water that engulfed the lower rooms.

By far, the most unusual feature of the house was the shower: when you wanted a hot shower all you had to do was flush the toilet twice. The water tank on the roof, where the sun had been beating down on it all day, provided hot water by lowering the water level to the heated water on top. You had to shower in the evening to ensure enough time had passed for the heating process. The alternative was to use the wood water heater when there was no sun.

Wood was in short supply, so the fuel source was dried corncobs, purchased cheaply from a vendor. The corncob merchant called out his wares as he led his little donkey up and down the cobblestone streets. Once a week, the garbage collector called out, *"basura"* along the same route. It was all quite simple and ingenious.

Me and My Magical Life

Because San Miguel de Allende attracted all kinds of people for various reasons, it was always a rather transient place. The young women of the courtyard house weren't there for long, so there was a constant need to advertise for housemates. While sitting outside the life drawing class waiting for the next session to begin, I met a woman from New York. She told me that she was looking for a place to live while a house was being prepared for her. The timing was perfect, and Betsy Dhursen moved into the courtyard house the next day.

I still laugh remembering our introduction to each other. The woman asked where I was from and what I was doing in San Miguel de Allende. When it was her turn, she told me that she was hiding out from a manic-depressive New York Harbor tugboat captain. That should have set off an alarm, but by then I realized every foreign visitor to Mexico had some amazing story to tell.

Soon another housemate joined us. Berris was a beautiful Australian woman who moved into the upstairs bedroom. She was a model in my life drawing class and made an impression because of the little bouquets of flowers that she tucked into her huge pierced ear holes whenever she went out. All of my drawings of Berris had flowers in her ears.

One balmy night, Berris and I were in bed asleep when we both awoke to the most awful noise in the courtyard. A group of people were singing off-key and shouting at the top of their lungs at three a.m. Just as I was about to crawl out of bed to investigate, the door to my room, which was off the courtyard, began to open slowly and I saw a hand groping for a light. I jumped up and shouted at the person, who made a hasty retreat back into the courtyard. As I stepped outside my door I saw Berris on the stairway, holding a two-by-four and threatening a drunk Mexican who was barely able to stand.

At that moment, Betsy stepped into view, and Berris and I realized Betsy and two men were stark naked. Betsy had picked up some guy in a bar, hired a taxi, and brought both men into our house so they could continue the party. We got rid of the intruders, put Betsy to bed, and made her promise never to bring men into the house in the middle of the night.

Fortunately, Betsy's house was soon ready, and after too many floods in the courtyard, Berris and I found separate housing elsewhere. I moved into a lovely modern house made entirely of rough stone, joining yet another pair of young women. The house was part of a compound that included a clay tennis court located a little distance from the Instituto.

Unlike in town, we had beautiful views of the countryside and a pleasant walk to school. As fate would have it, the house Betsy leased was just down the dirt road from us. I passed it nearly every morning when I walked to a tiny *tienda* where I bought eggs and fresh *bollios* (small oval rolls with a crunchy crust covering a divine soft dough). Sometimes the bollios were still warm, and I can still conjure up that heavenly aroma that followed me all the way home.

One hot sunny morning as I approached Betsy's house, I saw smoke billowing up from the courtyard, which was open to the road. The source of the fire was a mattress that had been thrown out an upstairs window. The house had a wrought iron fence about ten feet high that surrounded the property. The gate was locked so there was nothing I could do except stand there and shout Betsy's name. There was no response, so I figured she was either dead drunk, or dead, neither of which I could do anything about. When Betsy and I met a few days later she explained that she and some guy she picked up got really drunk and were shooting holes in the bedroom ceiling with a pistol. They passed out before extinguishing a burning cigarette.

It was a pattern I would observe over and over in one form or another. Betsy, when sober, was a wonderful woman. She told me she had attended the Art Students League in New York as a young woman and had been a friend of Jackson Pollock before his death. She also claimed Willem and Elaine de Kooning had been friends, and each of whom had given her paintings as gifts. According to Betsy the paintings were being kept by her eighty-two-year-old father, for her own good.

It was easy for me to appreciate her father's concern, because she was forever giving things away when under the influence. Betsy had a son, Andrew, who lived with her father. He was the same age as Julie and they happened to be visiting us at the same time. The teenagers spent a lot of time together, comparing notes about their quirky moms. According to Julie, Betsy won on that front.

All of the house moves took place in a short time, not unusual for a place like San Miguel de Allende. During that time, I had been visiting with a young woman from Houston who lived with her mother on Aldama Street, just behind the *Parroquia*, the huge cathedral directly across from the plaza. Rodda and I met in the *Jardin* every evening just after sunset and shared a bench for the sport of people watching. She was an extremely attractive young woman, with long ash-blond hair that Mexican men could barely resist touching. I served as an ersatz chaparone for the girl, and she helped me with Spanish and Mexican cultural explanations.

Charlotte Plantz

Until both men departed, Jimmy and John were almost always seated on the next bench. We referred to ourselves as the *Jardineros*, or people who sat on wrought iron benches so long they got permanent ridges in their butts. One evening, Rodda told me that her mother was moving back to Houston. She wanted to meet me about the possibility of my moving into their house so she would not have to worry about her daughter living there alone.

Nearly all the houses in San Miguel de Allende had high walls surrounding them, so you never knew what you might find after stepping through the door or gate. I was stunned as I was shown into Rodda and her mother's house, for it was simply beautiful. I entered a smallish living room, its floor covered with antique Navajo rugs. A bulldog was chewing on one corner of a rug, but that didn't seem to alarm the pair in the least.

A whole living room wall was glass and opened onto a courtyard with a large fountain in the center. The sound of splashing water covered much of the street noise, and then I noticed another fountain on a wall over two stories high that was covered with two different colors of bougainvillea: magenta and orange. It was an eye-popping sight.

The Aldama property was quite narrow and deep and completely enclosed by high walls. A dining room with a glass wall opened onto the courtyard, and was furnished with furniture made by Rodda's father, who had died just as the house was completed. There was a small powder room and a door into a small yet efficient kitchen that opened to a raised patio that overlooked the fountains and flowers galore. The patio had a fireplace, a refrigerator for drinks, and round leather tables and chairs for entertaining groups of twelve of more with adjustments. Behind the patio was the laundry: a flat cement basin with water, where clothes were pushed back and forth and then wrung out by hand. No easy feat when dealing with sheets and heavy towels. Next to that was a bathroom for Antonia, the *criada*, or maid. The last room in the courtyard was the workshop, where Rodda's father had built his furniture and applied gold leaf to a number of pieces.

My mouth was agape as Rodda continued her house tour, leading me upstairs to a landing with two bedrooms and a huge bathroom. That room had a big stained glass window that splattered color all over the room when the sun was just right. A third bedroom was reached by walking through the master bedroom, or from the balcony, where a door opened into that room at the very back of the house. Where the balcony ended, a spiral staircase led up to the flat roof, where we would spend many hours watching sunsets and huge flocks of jabbering grackles as they settled into purple flowering jacaranda trees for the night.

From the rooftop you could see the entire city center, which included Bellas Artes, an art school that specialized in the many crafts known throughout Mexico. Unlike the Instituto Allende, the Bellas Artes was taught in Spanish and the student body consisted primarily of Mexican students seeking to learn marketable skills. I once witnessed a nun being lifted off the Bellas Artes rooftop while she pulled a rope attached to a huge bell, announcing the time of day.

I had noticed during the tour that the house had amenities unheard of in most Mexican households: color television, electric blankets, and built-in reading lights for all the beds. Telephones upstairs and downstairs; every consideration had been made for comfort on a grand scale.

Charlotte Plantz

Antonia, the *criada*, came every morning at nine to prepare Rodda and Susan's breakfast. She then proceeded with the day's chores that included shopping for the comida that was served at two in the afternoon.

Antonia worked until five in the evening, six days a week. The gardener, Luis, came two days a week to work with the flowers and plants that were an integral part of the household. Bouquets of fresh flowers were in every room. Every now and then, a flower vendor friend of Antonia's stopped by with a huge tub of flowers that she carried on her head to and from the Instituto. If the woman hadn't sold all the flowers, the leftover bouquets were placed in the fountain until next morning, saving the woman a long walk with a heavy load.

Between the sounds of splashing water and the scent of flowers, life on Calle Aldama turned out to be quite a heady experience. Needless to say, I accepted the invitation to move in with Rodda. As soon as her mother headed back to Houston I moved into the back bedroom. The only cost to me was a share of the food expenses. I could hardly believe my good luck. For the next seven months, Rodda and I lived the good life and got on really well together. She, of all people, became the best Spanish teacher I had. Because Antonia spoke no English, I slowly learned to communicate within the household. It changed my life forever.

13
Living a Creative Life As a Single Woman

Summer quarter began the end of May and continued for ten weeks to the end of August. The previous year I had met a young woman at New Mexico Highlands University who was from Bangladesh. Her brother was starting a textile factory in that country, and Halide asked whether I was interested in working for him as a designer. My response had been that I lacked a formal background in that area even though I had been doing batik and other fabric arts for years.

Amazingly, when I read the Instituto Allende catalog and saw classes in textile design, the plan just worked itself out for me. I learned that a man named Bill Hinz from the Art Institute of Chicago was teaching that class during the summer quarter. Halide and I agreed that the timing might be perfect for me to study with him and then consider her brother's offer in Bangladesh. However, that never happened. Bangladesh entered into a long period of civil unrest, and Halide and her family fled to England.

Bill Hinz played a pivotal role in my earning a BFA degree from the Instituto Allende without ever paying a cent toward tuition. During the first week of Bill's class, he asked that we prepare a portfolio from the design assignments he gave us. From those, he would determine our skill level and base his teaching on the results. By the end of the next week, Bill had assessed our portfolios. He asked that I stay after class to talk with him. My design teacher told me he had learned that all my transferred money had been hung up somewhere, including my tuition. I was in fact selling some personal items to buy food.

The Instituto administrators told Hinz that he could offer me a fellowship as a teaching assistant and that would cover my tuition. The instructor said he was making the offer based on my portfolio, which he felt was quite original and professional. He said he would be pleased to have me as his assistant. I nearly fell over in delight. At summer's end, Bill once again kept me after class, and that time I had to hold on to the edge of a table as I heard him say that I was skilled enough to be teaching his class. And he had already recommended that very thing to Sterling Dickenson, the school president, and to Bill Parker, the dean of students. I met with those men shortly after that conversation. When I entered Bill Parker's office, another person was present. It was none other than Nell Fernandez, the owner of the Instituto Allende.

Nell was notorious for her flamboyance and facelifts. Though she was in her late seventies, she appeared much younger. During my three years in San Miguel de Allende, Nell could be spotted numerous evenings in nightclubs, dancing the night away, usually with much younger men: both foreign and local. Originally from Alabama, she had married the governor of the state of Guanajuato. Nell and the governor established the Instituto Allende in the nineteen thirties. After her husband's death, the widow retained enough political power to run the school in any way she saw fit.

Me and My Magiecal Life

After World War II, the school became accredited so returning GIs could attend and receive bona fide degrees. The Instituto had been attracting art aficionados ever since. Nell was incredibly astute in offering courses geared toward tourists, as well as maintaining the degree programs for more serious study. The school was divided into two main sections: the School of Fine Art, and the School of Crafts. It also offered a writing course taught by top-notch writers, and a Spanish program offering short intensive sessions as well as the degree program. All in all, the Instituto offered something for just about everyone. It was a creative magnet for people from around the world, and I was thrilled to be invited into the process.

For all my outer show of bravado, I was, in fact, a woman fraught with insecurities. Just being in the presence of the administrators, especially Nell, who also had a reputation for explosive outbursts, nearly had me nailed to the floor. Somehow, I sat there in a creaky leather chair, displaying nothing but calm assurance. We chatted a bit about what I would teach: fabric printing. The class would be offered three hours, three days a week. I was concerned that I would be replacing Judy Roberts, who had been teaching the class for years, but they assured me that Judy wanted to make a change and was in favor of my taking on her position.

With that, Nell spoke directly to me, saying that they would pay me a salary as well as free tuition. She pointed out it was something the school had never offered before. I could tell the gesture had been discussed beforehand with the two men, both of whom nodded agreeably as she spoke. I could hardly breathe hearing that news. To this day, I have no idea why that was offered to me, but I was determined to live up to it.

Charlotte Plantz

For me, it was another display of magic in my life. By the end of that summer quarter I was asked to teach another class in fabric design and was even given a raise. Unheard of! And teach I did. At the same time, I was carrying more than a full credit load. For the three years I spent at the Instituto I carried between sixteen and twenty units a quarter, allowing me to graduate with a BFA.

It could never have happened without Rodda and Antonia, and my life in the house on Calle Aldama. Living in a house with a full-time maid seemed awkward at first, but it did not take long for me to ease into the rhythm of that lifestyle. Especially, coming home from school for the midday break that is known throughout Mexico and Latin America as siesta and finding the main meal of the day already being prepared.

I taught three mornings, three hours, from nine to twelve, then attended my Spanish class from twelve to one, arriving home about one fifteen. There was just enough time to lie down for a rest until *comida* was announced at two, always at two, never earlier or later, no matter what. Antonia had a daily routine that included shopping for the day's meal. That trip included stops along the way to chat with friends, and she was not about to give that up.

Because I was a slow eater, it was after two thirty when I finished, so Rodda and I usually chatted until time for me to leave for the afternoon classes that resumed at three. My teaching schedule was based around classes that I needed to attend toward my degree: some were one-hour sessions, three times a week, such as art history, pre-Columbian history, Mexican art history, and an aesthetics class. There were other three-hour studio classes: ceramics, leather, weaving, or perhaps a jewelry class, not all at once, but spread out over the three years.

Me and My Magiecal Life

We were in school six days a week, and the afternoon classes lasted until six p.m. Fortunately for me, Antonia came on Saturdays as well, so all my personal needs were taken care of on a grand scale. My freshly washed and ironed clothes were always put away in drawers or closets. Evening snacks were available from the extra fridge on the patio. For three years I did absolutely nothing except teach and study. And, the best of all-create. As long as the weather was warm, Rodda and I continued our evening socializing in the *Jardin*. One class seemed to pile up on top of another until by the end of the second quarter I had amassed enough units to give me a glimpse of my future. My transferred money eventually arrived, though the tuition check never did. Having an income made it possible for me to save a bit.

The Instituto closed mid November for a six-week winter break. The other quarter breaks lasted two weeks, usually just enough time to dash to the border to renew my tourist visa and to rest a bit before resuming the grueling class schedule. I do not think I mentioned it before, but I was working in Mexico as an illegal, as were most of the teachers. We were paid every Friday with cash in tiny brown envelopes we picked up in a room in back of the mailboxes.

One Friday just as I entered the room, I saw Nell Fernandez standing with her back to me. She turned and began yelling at me to get out. I nearly fainted on the spot, until I realized she was talking with two men who I later learned were with the government. Nell later apologized, explaining that they were the feared *politicos* who could make trouble for all of us "illegals."

I tried once going to Mexico City to get proper papers, but the man in charge told me that if I were given legal status, my life would become a living nightmare.

He held his finger to his lips, whispering that he would pretend I had never entered his office. I didn't have the courage to try that again and continued to slink into the back room every Friday, praying it would be empty of Nell and Los Ojos.

By November, the entire teaching staff was relieved to be free of the energy required for pretense. It seemed strange to be buying a roundtrip ticket in reverse, but by then my life was pretty much on automatic. I knew that I had to be back at the Instituto by January 3 to resume teaching and studying. It was actually a marvelous feeling knowing that I had established myself as a single woman in a foreign country, with goals and ambitions being fulfilled, all within six months.

I had planned to take the train to the States, since it was much cheaper than flying. Just a few days before I bought my ticket, the phone rang and to my absolute amazement, it was Murray. I could not imagine how he tracked me down at Rodda's house, because we had had no contact since my arrival in Mexico. Murray had disappeared from the face of the earth according to his father.

Back on my first day at the Instituto in May, I had received a phone message from Murray's father in Florida, asking me to call him collect. He said he and his wife, Molly, had not heard from their son in over five months. The last time they had talked with Murray he told them where I was going, and that I refused to allow him to join me, even though he wanted to study photography at the Instituto.

Les asked whether he could fly down and join me in hopes that their son would ignore my objections and simply show up, as was his usual style. I couldn't believe I had the courage to stand up to that powerful, wealthy man and tell him that I had to do my life completely alone, free of all entanglements, even their concern for their son. I promised that I would call them the minute I heard from Murray, but beyond that there was nothing more I could do.

So there he was, the missing son, on the telephone, calling from his parents' winter townhouse in Tucson. At that moment all I thought about was scolding him for causing his parents so much grief. I made him promise to phone them the moment he hung up, and I made the same promise to myself, just in case. I had to laugh when I told Murray that I was leaving for California in a couple of days by train. He already knew that I could switch midpoint and wind up in Nogales, south of Tucson.

Since Murray could charm a snake, I was easy by comparison. Besides that, I was so fond of him and his prescient ways that I could not turn him down. It would be good to see him again, and especially to find out what he had been up to during his long disappearance. We agreed he would pick me up at the border crossing in Nogales a few days later. I phoned his parents the minute we hung up and their relief was audible.

I was meeting up with a group of students from the Instituto who were also heading back to the States for the holidays. We would actually meet on the train because they were leaving from Mexico City, and I was departing from Guadalajara. I had several baskets packed with Christmas gifts and two bags of clothing, so after two long bus rides I took a taxi to the train depot, where I thought I was checking my baggage onto the train. Baggage-free, I headed off for a visit to the huge indoor market not far from the station. I got back in plenty of time, feeling proud of myself for being so organized, boarded the train, and found the students.

Charlotte Plantz

Only when I arrived in Nogales and began looking for my luggage did I learn that I had been responsible for getting bags on to the train. All my belongings were left behind in Guadalajara, and I was quite sure, never to be seen again. I had nothing but a change of underwear and two Spanish books in a little cloth bag. The next shock was that the train station was in the middle of nowhere.

By the time the students and I had pursued every possibility for finding my bags, all the buses and taxis had departed, leaving us behind with no transportation out. Because they were young and adventurous, the students hustled us out onto a highway, where we stuck out our thumbs, hitching a ride. Within minutes a hippie in a van pulled up and we piled in for the ride to the border.

Murray was waiting for me in his blue Jeep, and as I told my travel story, our sides were splitting from laughter by the time we pulled up to the house. Little did I know that my lost bags were just the beginning, for when he unlocked the door and we stepped inside, my first awareness was that all the rooms were empty of furniture. All I could see were two bar stools at a counter in the kitchen. The surprise on my face brought gales of laughter from Murray, who took my hand and led me into the kitchen. He stopped in front of the sink, where he pointed to something just below, explaining that all was not lost, since there was a dishwasher and a trash compactor!

I spent a week in Tucson, studying Spanish from the two books I brought and washing the one change of underclothing, while Murray worked at a camera store. I also walked a lot and tried not to think too much, taking advantage of the time to physically rest before the next phase of life would propel me into action. In addition to the kitchen appliances, the Lundberg condo contained two sets of twin bed mattresses and box springs that lay on the floor of an upstairs bedroom. Murray had one set of sheets, so he took the fitted one and gave me the other, plus one of the two blankets, saying if it got too cold we could just turn up the heat, unlike in Chacon, where you had to keep a fire going or freeze to death.

The morning after my arrival, I was sitting on the john, wearing what I thought was Murray's T-shirt, but the hem had rolled up, and printed in neat block letters was the name Mike Plantz. I started laughing as I emerged from the bathroom and hollered at Murray, who was in the kitchen making coffee. I moved toward him, holding the edge of the T-shirt with both hands. He asked what I found so funny at that time of morning, and I replied that I might have just been given a "sign." Wouldn't it be strange if Mike Plantz and I fell in love and got married?

I suddenly realized that Murray knew nothing of my visit with Mike seven months earlier. I waited until that night before we went to bed to tell Murray about Mike and our time together. We lay in the dark talking, and were both comforted by the ease between us in such a setting. It was the umpteenth time I had compared such situations to having girlfriends when I was younger.

From the first time Mike, Murray, and I had shared a bedroom in Chacon, I had felt like the luckiest woman in the world. Those were literally slumber parties with men, free of even the slightest hint of sexual innuendo between us, even though sometimes we talked about sex. After living so many years in a world of sexual intrigue and deception, I could not think of anything healthier, than sharing a room and intimate conversation with Mike and Murray. As naive as that sounded, we all believed the world would be a better place if everyone could get that concept.

Charlotte Plantz

Murray was stunned to learn that Mike and I might have feelings stronger than friendship between us. But as I pointed out to him, life was full of twists and turns and until something really happened, he should not concern himself with that possibility. Especially since Mike and I had no clue where we might be headed. Laughing, I added that Mike Plantz was probably the only man in the universe who could tolerate having Murray burst in on his life, no matter who the woman was.

And then it was time for me to leave for California. Murray drove me to the airport, and that time he did not hassle me about Mexico. It felt like my young friend had matured some and had begun to think about his own life choices. As it turned out I was right, for soon Murray moved to Taos and fell in love with a young woman named Patricia. She was a wonderful mother to two young boys and a photographer. It was a perfect match because Murray became devoted to Sam and his brother and shared his love of photography with their mother. We didn't see each other again until the following year, and that was in Taos under very different circumstances.

14
Home for the Holidays

Going home for the holidays was a bittersweet experience. It was wonderful to be with my daughters again, but sad that my family had written me off as a lost cause. There would be no holiday family gathering that included us. But in some ways it was also liberating, because past family gatherings had become contentious affairs, with too much alcohol being consumed by my parents. That always led to grousing and sniping and a pattern of somebody being put in the "out" position. As long as I can remember, in our family somebody always had to be singled out for that role. Over the years, as I began to pay attention, it dawned on me how destructive that pattern had become.

I don't believe there was ever a time in my adult life when we were all united, especially us siblings. But then, as I learned later, that was precisely the object of the game that we referred to as "odd guy out." It had been going on for years and the older we grew, the nastier the process became. It was one of the reasons I left the state when I divorced. I knew that a bad marriage was not my only problem, because I found myself more and more in the dreaded position of "odd guy out."

I had been a psychology buff for years, so I was aware that something was wrong within our family.

Charlotte Plantz

The more I tried to talk about it with my siblings, the more I found myself being singled out as the problem. The only reasonable solution was to remove myself from the playing field, for by then, it was a matter of survival.

After more than ten years of therapy with the kindest, most astute psychiatrist, I learned that my mother probably suffered a mental illness known as borderline personality disorder. I did a lot of reading and research on the disorder and came to the conclusion that it is one of the most destructive personalities on earth. Research shows that the disorder is probably brought on by traumas early in childhood. From the stories we heard growing up, that fit our mother's background precisely.

Our grandmother had married five times in an era when divorce was nearly unheard of. Mother's father, whom she adored, ran off to San Francisco to become an opera singer when she was five years old. He was never heard from again. From then on, my mother became the victim of stepfathers who abused her physically and sexually.

After Mother graduated from high school, she ran away from two incredible career possibilities offered by her mother. She was sent to Chicago to study opera, but instead got right back on the train to Kansas. The following year she was sent to Chicago again, that time to study nursing. Once again, my mother turned around and headed home to play basketball on the town team. She met our father during the depths of the Depression and Dust Bowl, when she was twenty-one. They married, and I was born the first year.

It was apparent to all that my parents adored one another. With no birth control, there would be three more children, the last one, a sister, on my fifteenth birthday. We always had a piano so the house was filled with music. Every evening the family joined around the piano, and we sang for entertainment. Mother began to voice her regret at not following her opera dream, and as the years passed, bitter disappointment began to take its toll.

By the time we children entered our teenage years, as in most families, a power struggle began in earnest. I noticed that my mother had a benign way of seducing my friends away from me. The next thing I knew, my friends were coming to spend time with my mother, and I felt sidelined, with the exception of my childhood sister friends who never fell into her web. As a result, to the end of her life, my mother never liked them and badmouthed the girls and their parents (who had been good friends for a long time).

Abandonment plays a pivotal role in borderline personality disorder, so the sufferer becomes adept at intricate ploys to keep that from happening to them. Keeping her children divided was essential to that end, so our mother became expert in that area. It grew worse as we married and had children of our own, because there were more people for Mother to divide, even if they were children. Over time, the intensity of the game became even more magnified.

Our mother's only defense was to ensure that we did not like each other. That included our spouses and children, for again, in her eyes, if we ever united, the unspeakable was sure to happen. The unspeakable for her was to have us care for one another and join forces as a united front against her. As I grew to understand what was taking place, I tried to explain it to my siblings. But because we had been taught to dislike and distrust one another, it just made me the "bad guy out."

By then, I pretty much chose to move out of the situation physically as well as mentally. As I explained to my daughters a long time before my divorce, somebody simply had to do something to break the horrible cycle of destruction. It had become impossible to live a happy life within that destructive belief system that impacted all our lives.

Eventually, the four of us siblings did unite and we staged an intervention with our mother. We asked her to choose a mediator that she felt comfortable with. She chose her Presbyterian minister. The day before the intervention, my siblings and I spent the night in a hotel and talked into the night. For the first time in our lives we compared notes and shared experience of being made the "bad guy out" by our mother and father, who was also being manipulated by her.

Our only brother in some ways suffered the worst of it because Mother hated his wife. She openly taunted and tormented Shirley in front of their children and anyone who happened to be present. The intervention did not go well. In fact, it made our lives worse because it kicked Mother into a higher level of viciousness. The poor clergyman was so shaken by the event he couldn't move for a while. He asked us to stay and try to explain our mother's behavior, because he had never experienced anything like what had just taken place.

I was sixty-two years old before I was able to tell my mother that even though I loved her, I was unable to allow her to affect my life with her destructive behavior. Telephone calls had become verbal battles. It was like trying to make my way through a minefield, and there was no way I could come out unscathed. Mother was happiest when I was down, because I was vulnerable. If I were in a good space or seemed especially happy, the game began in earnest. In her mind, she could not tolerate someone's joy or contentment. She had become so skilled at manipulation there was no way you could outmaneuver her.

During the last telephone conversation with my mother, all those years ago, she was at one of her high points in destructive plotting. As I hung up I began to feel strange physically, and I stepped outside on the porch for fresh air. When I stepped off the porch I became so disoriented that I tripped on a rock and literally went reeling across the front of the house. Subconsciously, I was searching for a place to make a safe landing, because it was apparent I was going to fall forward. Our yard consisted of rocky packed adobe, so my hope was for landing in a flowerbed with softer earth. It all happened in slow motion, and I felt clear-headed regarding my impending fall. I just kept bending lower and lower to the ground, with my center of gravity pulling me down.

I did fall in the flowerbed, but not before scraping my knees on the rock border and mashing my chin into the earth. I thought I had broken both wrists since I had stuck out my hands to break the fall. I started screaming at the top of my lungs, and when I was finally able to get myself up I could not stop shaking. At that moment, I vowed my mother would never, ever affect me that way again. I was sixty-two years old and had finally had enough.

The next day I sat down and wrote five letters to my mother before I had one that would be tolerable to send. I told her that I could only communicate through the mail because our conversations threatened my mental and physical health. When I told my psychiatrist what I had done, he leaped out of his chair, shouting, "You're cured!" Even though I had been dealing with a nuisance-level bipolar disorder for years, the "cycle of destruction" or "cycle of evil," as the doctor called it, had been broken.

Charlotte Plantz

I was definitely cured of that. Any time you become acutely aware of destructive behavior that affects you and you choose to ignore it, you become the victim by default. Only you have the power to change it. And as they say: Better Late Than Never!

15
Memorable Christmas on the North Coast

I arrived home in time for Thanksgiving so it was good to throw myself into holiday activities. The girls were still in school, so once again we fell into our old routine with school friends dropping in for conversations. We sat around the kitchen table for hours, and it was great fun to share my halting Spanish and stories of Mexico and the wonderful people I had met. Both girls had come to San Miguel de Allende for visits at separate times during the seven months I was there, so we had many shared experiences to talk about.

A letter from Mike Plantz was waiting for me when I arrived. He wrote that he had his own apartment in Eureka, one street over from his sister and her family. He was working again for Simpson Timber lumber mill on the evening shift and hoped that I would come up for a visit before returning to Mexico on January 1. I wrote Mike to arrange a telephone call at his sister's so we could talk about a visit later in December. And then I began to panic.

Even though Mike and I had been writing one another the past few months, the reality of being together physically took my breath away. Part of me wanted no attachments of any kind. I wanted to get my degree as quickly as possible and return to some kind of normal life back in the States. However, I had never known anyone like Mike. We shared so many things on so many levels it was hard to ignore the possibility of what might lay ahead for us.

With that in mind, we picked two weeks before Christmas for my visit, with an arrival on Saturday since he had the weekend off. For the second time that year, I set out for Humboldt County and another adventure in uncertainty. I was astounded by the weather, for December on the North Coast of California could be daunting. Huge storms often triggered flooding and mudslides that made driving a challenge. Mike told me that when he moved north in 1970 it rained from October until March, when the sun finally came out.

Amazingly, the weather was clear and sunny, even slightly warm for a change. That drive had me jumpy, but not from fear of the elements; it was fear of the romantic unknown. I knew that having his own apartment meant things would be different between Mike and me. We had both touched on that possibility after our last visit seven months earlier.

By the time I reached Eureka around three in the afternoon, I was a nervous wreck. I arrived at Mike's apartment on Washington Street only to find it empty. I could not believe it. I thought maybe he had changed his mind and didn't want to see me after all. Fortunately his sister, Sue, was at home on the next street and seemed delighted to see me. I mumbled something about not being sure why I had come, and she replied that it was a good thing I did, or her brother would be beside himself with grief. That made me feel better and I began to relax.

Sue said Mike had gone to the beach to watch the sunset and would return shortly. The two of us had tea and chatted until the light began to fade. By then I was getting nervous again. Finally I said I had to go see whether he had returned, because I might turn around and drive back to Folsom that night.

Mike's car was parked in front of the apartment house, so I knew he had returned. There was a little foyer with a staircase that led to the apartment above. I knocked on his door and waited a long time before realizing I could hear a shower running on the other side of the wall. I waited until the water was shut off and then knocked again. It took a bit before Mike got his clothes on and finally opened the door. We stood there for a while and then instinctively reached for one another.

To this day, Mike and I both agree we heard bells and saw fireworks as we stood locked in that embrace. We didn't kiss, we just held on to each other for what seemed like an eternity. When I finally opened my eyes and looked into the living room, I saw a bed, a double bed on one side of the room. I yelped, "A bed. You have a bed in your living room." Mike pulled me into the room and shut the door, laughing. I was sure he was concerned about his neighbors. Still laughing nervously, he said we would be going to dinner at his sister's and I should not worry about the bed.

I tried not to worry about the bed, but the image stayed with me as we ate our meal with Sue and her family. It was wonderful being with them again, and I especially enjoyed the children, who were adorable. The youngest, Becky, had turned two since we last met, and she wanted to draw for me. I was astounded by the results: the child drew stick figures, but they had eyelashes and fingers and toes. Becky had autism and spent a lot of time sitting on top of the dryer beneath a plastic laundry basket, sometimes quietly, but other times screaming endlessly. Poor Sue had her hands full with Becky but seemed incredibly patient and understanding.

The other children were loving and considerate with their sister. Sue's husband, Dale, was thoughtful and jovial, and especially good with the children. It was a pleasant experience and we all enjoyed ourselves. Sue adored Mike and was thrilled that he might have a romantic interest. Mike had been married for a month five years earlier, but after an annulment there hadn't been another woman. When I met Mike in Chacon that summer, I thought that he must be in hiding from a tortured romantic interest. Little did any of us know that he was waiting for the right woman to turn up in his life.

It was after ten when Mike and I said goodnight to his family and walked around the block to his apartment. When he opened the door I began to shake. Mike said I should sit in a big overstuffed chair while he poured us drinks of tequila that he had bought in honor of the occasion. He sat facing me in another chair as we sipped the fiery liquor straight. I told him I thought I should drive back to Folsom and he started laughing, reminding me it was a three-hundred-mile drive in the middle of the night. Mike said that I should try to relax, especially because we had shared rooms before. That did help, but then I jumped up, saying I really had to go.

And then I broke out in hives, from my left shoulder down my arm to my hand. Mike jumped up too and began to pet my arm, trying to make the hives go away. The two of us were like strips of Velcro jumping around, trying to fit together. We both started laughing as he continued to gently massage my arm. Then we were kissing, and then we were on the bed with clothes flying all over the room. Forty-six years later, we swear that we were married on the spot.

Me and My Magical Life

The next morning, the two of us walked a few blocks to Denny's for breakfast. When the waitress came with menus, she looked from one to the other of us and asked, "Did you guys just get married or something?" We took that as a "sign" and for the next three years, Mike had stars shooting out of his eyes. I was not the only one to notice. In Mexico people sometimes stopped us on the street because of those shooting stars. Everyone agreed they had never seen such a happy man newly in love.

Amazing how a person can be one thing one day, then wake up and be something entirely different the next. That is what falling in love did. Everything on earth changed, or at least that was the perception. The next day, Mike and I looked at one another and declared, "Oh my God, now what do we do?" Because Mike had always been an incredibly pragmatic kind of guy, he decided that we must take it one day at a time. However, I knew I was committed to teaching two classes in Mexico in a few weeks. After all I had been through I felt that I couldn't walk away from my life there.

Sue came to our rescue by announcing that their parents and brother were flying up from southern California to spend a few days for Christmas. She suggested that I drive back to Folsom and return with Julie and Cyndi so we could celebrate the holiday season together. Sue and Dale thought it was apparent that Mike and I had just married. Though we lacked the formal ceremony, they thought we should celebrate the union. That was what we needed to propel us into action.

However, the thought of being separated for any length of time was nearly unbearable. The fear of loss loomed huge in our imaginations. I drove back to Folsom but everything was different; the route felt warm and familiar. I was so full of love every bend in the road appeared to bathe the little car in dazzling shafts of light. Colors were brighter, the sky bluer, and the weather calm and serene. So much like Mike that now and then I would shiver with desire. The drive became a bittersweet journey for me. I experienced a vast array of emotions and had time to savor those feelings all the way home. I could hardly wait to share my joy with my daughters.

I arrived shortly after nine p.m. to find the girls waiting for me. They were indeed thrilled and excited, but not too surprised since I had phoned them several times during my week with Mike. Julie and Cyndi were especially pleased to be going on a trip while a bit apprehensive about landing in the midst of an entire extended family for Christmas. Viewing the trip as another adventure, we threw ourselves into shopping for small gifts for Mike and his family and prepared to leave within a day or two. Julie was excited because she took over some of the driving, and the trip expanded her world even more.

My father had been such a marvelous adventurer presence in my life I had always wanted my daughters to experience that same thrill of the unknown. I hoped they would never be afraid of venturing into uncharted territory. A recent conversation with my younger sister brought up an old family story about me as a three-year-old riding in the front seat of our father's taxicab. As the story goes, I was the apple of my father's eye and he loved taking me to work with him, whether it was at his butcher shop or driving a taxi in a small Kansas town, circa 1939.

My father was known for his kindness and progressive philosophy; he had lived with a black family for a while at age ten after his parents' divorce, so I grew up without prejudice of any kind. My grandfather had a reputation as an adventurer as well and had been a bootlegger when he and my dad, who was twelve, lived in Rocky Ford, Colorado. Grandpa Ross was also a manager at the local Coca-Cola bottling plant, so he straddled two different worlds as my father was growing up.

One of Dad's stories was about hopping a freight train with a group of other boys when he was eleven and nearly freezing to death. In fact, one boy did die from the cold, and that cured my dad of riding the rails and living life as a hobo into adulthood. Instead, he joined a circus as a roustabout and lived with the freak show characters as they traveled the circuit.

We heard those stories growing up, sitting around the dining table with our eyes wide open; taking in every word. My father never lived with his mother again and instead joined the CCC (Civilian Conservation Corps), which employed young men during the Depression. He also joined the cavalry and became a superb horseman and went on to ride Brahma bulls in rodeos. Dad made up country and western songs and could yodel with the best of them. All in all, my father was a wonderful adventure unto himself, and he shared that with the four of us siblings, though I would become the most adventurous of the lot.

And that takes me back to the taxicab story: one summer my father picked up a man who had no legs. The man loved to swim and my father was the only way that could happen. With me in the front seat of the taxi, my father went inside the man's house and put him on his back. He carried the man to the taxi and then into the town swimming pool. He actually set the man down in the water and watched him swim away like a fish. Those trips took place often, and I know being witness to the events shaped my life view. It was also a guarantee that I would never meet a stranger.

Charlotte Plantz

Compared to my daughters' New Mexico experience the previous year, a trip to northern California was actually pretty tame. Blessed with continued mild weather, my daughters were awed by the beauty of the landscape as we journeyed north. Sue and Dale had insisted that they had enough room and beds for everyone so that Mike and I could spend our few remaining nights together in the little no-bedroom apartment. For us, that was the best Christmas gift of all, and we were extremely grateful.

We would surely know by the end of March whether we wanted to spend the rest of our lives together. At the time we could not imagine an alternative. That must be one of the gifts of falling in love later in life.

Sue and Dale embraced Julie and Cyndi into their family, and as I had known they would, the girls fell in love with their little children. Davy, Jenny, and Becky were in heaven with so much attention and with the beautiful Christmas tree and all the excitement of the holiday. The house was filled with wonderful smells as the women fell into a natural rhythm of cooking together. It did have the feel of a wedding as well, because Mike's entire family had been waiting for years for the shy bachelor to find the woman of his dreams. We laughed about shooting stars, and every face glowed. Christmas dinner was a traditional affair, and I had never seen anybody whip mashed potatoes into perfection by hand as Mike's father did.

All too soon the festivities came to an end, and it was time to head back down Highway 101, but not before a few days of sightseeing and playing on the beaches in the cold winter air. Julie and Cyndi had never been on the North Coast before, and it gave the four of us an opportunity to do some bonding. Mike proved to be a

Me and My Magical Life

thoughtful tour guide as he led us through his favorite haunts.

And then we headed south with a new driver. Mike had decided to accompany us in order to spend a few more days together. Once I was on the plane for Mexico, he would take a Greyhound bus home on New Year's Day. We had phoned ahead to inform Fabian that Mike would be staying over a couple of days, and once again my ex-husband proved to be flexible and considerate. However, he came to the house once while Mike was there, I was sure out of curiosity. Amusingly or alarmingly, once there, Fabian said he needed to pick up his shotgun.

Mike had never been to our Folsom house and enjoyed the experience because his childhood friend, Barry McWilliams had visited us on numerous occasions. Mike had heard some of the stories and was able to make a visual connection. And then it was time for us to go our separate ways and it was like being ripped apart, when what we wanted was to be stuck together like Velcro. The one consolation for us both was the incredible love we felt for one another. Mike stated, "The realization that when you find your perfect half, there is simply no doubt." We parted with that thought firmly embedded in our minds, and it sustained us during the next three months.

16
Three Long Months

I needed to return to the train station in Guadalajara to see whether my belongings were still there. Talk on the plane was of the possibility of revolution in Mexico. I had heard some of that among the *Jardineros* in San Miguel before going back to the States. The year was 1974 and there were rumors of a large guerrilla band living in the hills surrounding Guadalajara. One of my students swore she had dated one of the revolutionaries, and he told her some of their plans. A bank had just been bombed in the city where I would land. I did experience some anxiety as I crossed the tarmac, especially because I had just found the love of my life. That feeling of impending loss would haunt me for months.

But at that moment there were other factors to be dealt with, so I quickly hailed a taxi and headed for the train station. I approached the baggage counter and displayed the receipt stubs given me at the time of my departure, six weeks earlier. The man in charge excused himself and retreated to another room. He returned shortly, and to my utter amazement, he was carrying two of my bags. By then he was smiling broadly, as he excused himself again to retrieve the remaining baskets.

On some level I had kept the faith that my things would still be there for me, but then again, it was Mexico.

Charlotte Plantz

I held a deep-seated belief that the very word Mexico conjured up dishonesty. My face flushed slightly at the thought. The baggage man was still smiling as he stood before me, obviously relieved that I had returned to find everything in order.

I tried to explain that I thought after my bags were checked in they would be put on the train. He smiled again, nodding, and told me that a lot of foreigners thought the same, but usually discovered their error in plenty of time. We both laughed as he explained that I would have to pay "rent" for the month and a half the luggage languished in the storage room. My smile suddenly faded because I thought that he was asking for a *mordida*, or bribe for his services. But just as quickly, the man produced a paper showing the daily rate for storage.

The fee was small, not over five dollars. By then, I was delighted to pay for the safe care of my personal belongings. I thanked the man profusely, shook hands with him, and piled everything onto a luggage cart and went in search of a taxi to take me to the bus station.

By the time I walked out of the station it was dusk and I was ravenous, thankful for food vendors on the sidewalk in front. I knew about the risks of eating on the streets but figured I would take a chance, especially since everything else had fallen into place for me that day. It was hardly a nuisance to be hauling all that stuff back to San Miguel. I realized that it had to do with the baggage man, and my belief in honesty and the goodness of mankind. I took a first-class bus to the little city of Celaya, a distance of about one hundred thirty miles. From Celaya, I had to transfer to another bus for the thirty-mile ride to San Miguel de Allende. My bus arrived in Celaya around midnight, and I was dismayed to learn that there were no buses running until morning.

Me and My Magical Life

I sat in the empty station surrounded by my bags and baskets. I was exhausted but incredibly happy and filled with love. I felt no fear of the world whatsoever. Just before five a.m., the ticket seller called me over to the counter. He told me that a fourth-class bus would be heading out for San Miguel de Allende shortly. He said there would not be a first-class bus until seven a.m., so without hesitation I bought my ticket and hauled the baggage onto the sidewalk-just as the bus pulled up.

Mexican buses always have two men on board: a driver and his helper, who sits in the seat behind the driver. A year later, Mike and I wondered about that tradition, until we were in Celaya shopping. We had caught the last bus out at dusk. The bus was packed to the roof with people standing, and we had to stash our groceries beneath the driver's seat. Mike and I had to hold on to each other as the bus careened around curves in the growing darkness. At one point the headlights began to blink on and off but the driver never even slowed down.

Finally, as everyone began to show signs of terror, the bus stopped alongside the road. The assistant driver got up on the hood and lay flat, banging on the lights as the bus driver proceeded, at last more slowly. That's how we discovered the real role of the assistant driver, especially on second, third, and fourth-class buses.

So there I was, on a fourth-class bus and another new experience. The bus had broken windows so the cold morning air rushed in and revived me from my groggy state. By then, I had been up nearly twenty-four hours. There were also holes in the floor, so you had to pick your seat carefully.

When I boarded the bus three men also got on, one of whom chose to sit in the seat next to me. Thinking about the revolution, I got out my tobacco pouch, rolled a cigarette, and offered it to him. He smiled appreciatively as he accepted my gift, and I made one for myself. The two of us sat there with cold air pouring in from all sides, enjoying the simple act of sharing a habit.

A while later, the bus stopped abruptly in the middle of nowhere, two men got on. It was pitch black, with not a light anywhere in the distance. How the driver saw them was a mystery, but even more mysterious was that they were carrying rifles-in a country where it was against the law to carry arms.

The revolution drifted into my imagination again, and I remembered seeing a lot of graffiti on walls in Celaya that dealt with social issues. The growing number of male passengers smiled at me and I rolled more cigarettes as we chatted about America and Mexico. A couple of the men had worked in the States as "illegals" but swore they only wanted to make enough money to live in their beloved country.

By the time the sun was peeking over the hills, the bus was nearly half full, with most of the men holding rifles upright between their knees. I decided if there was a revolution I was in the right place. At the next stop a young man from the Instituto got on and sat near me. He was amused that I was the only woman on the bus and having animated conversations with the rest of the passengers. By then, they were getting off in the middle of nowhere-just the way they had entered.

January in San Miguel de Allende was an entirely new experience. It was cold. The altitude of nearly seven thousand feet brought near-freezing temperatures at night. That explained the electric blankets on all the beds that I had found puzzling when I arrived at Rodda's house. The only way to heat the house was the small kiva fireplace in the living room. It was cozy and romantic sitting in front of the fire, but otherwise totally inadequate.

I asked Antonia how she had been during my absence. The young woman had a disturbing response. She said that her family nearly froze to death, despite sleeping four to a bed. Antonia's family had also suffered a food shortage that turned the cold spell into a health hazard. I realized just how poor Antonia and her family were, along with most of the people in that country. I had little money myself, but somehow I was able to travel a bit and live in a foreign place. Antonia and most of her countrymen had virtually no alternatives. The contrast would haunt me until I left Mexico for good.

I learned a vital lesson teaching a fabric printing class during the morning sessions in January. The dyes didn't work properly due to the icy water flowing from the taps. There was no hot water in the building where I taught. During warm months that presented no problem; however, since most of the dye processes I used required vast amounts of water, I had to come up with a new lesson plan. Thankfully, I had always been a quick-change artist so I came up with a whole new winter project.

Winter quarter was traditionally the time of year when retired New Yorkers descended upon the Instituto like locusts. My classes were full to the brim with exuberant women and an occasional man, eager to learn all they could within a short time. I scheduled a field trip to the little city of Dolores Hidalgo, renowned for its beautiful hand-painted tiles.

The city was also known for the multitude of homemade ice cream vendors surrounding the jardin. Each vendor stood behind an ingenious apparatus that consisted of a large stainless-steel cylinder set in a big tub of ice. A wood pole stuck up from the center of the cylinder.

Charlotte Plantz

When spun between the hands of the salesman, the wood paddles churned the ice cream. You could buy: avocado ice cream, cheese ice cream, and ice cream flavored with the exotic fruits of the country. The ice cream vendors were a big tourist draw and their products worth the trip.

I had instructed my students to choose one simple tile design of no more than three colors for our new project. My plan was to silk-screen the designs onto fabric using a simple technique that required nothing more than wooden embroidery hoops, pieces of nylon organdy, and diluted Elmer's Glue, all readily available and cheap. From that humble assemblage the students set to work, creating some lovely results. A few people printed enough fabric to be used as bed covers by using a chalk grid on large pieces of fabric.

A class in fabric design grew out of that project, and cold weather ceased to be a problem. I requested that my winter classes be held during the afternoons, and that made everyone happy. I loved the fluidity of the Instituto more than anything and felt that was one of the reasons it worked so well creatively. It made me feel more secure in my choice of the school for my own education.

Winter was a productive time for me. It was my most creative period, so I loaded myself up with classes and worked harder than ever. In a way it was easier because social life tended to slow down as people hunkered down just trying to stay warm. Mike and I were writing each other often, but many of his letters never reached me due to the Mexican postal service. I always wondered where those letters landed. Mike had sent a tape of guitar music he played for me, and that one never made it either. At times, I thought perhaps he had lost interest in our relationship, but I was still extremely insecure. Just when I started to believe that, a letter

Me and My Magical Life

would arrive, reassuring me once more that love was indeed alive.

One evening mid-February I was sitting in the local movie theatre watching an American film dubbed in Spanish with English subtitles, a rather strange experience. All of a sudden I was thrust up out of my seat and nearly ran all the way home. I missed Mike so much I could hardly stand it. I phoned his sister, praying he might be there, and amazingly he was.

When I heard his voice I started to shake, and laugh, and cry, as I tried to tell him how much I loved him. I just wanted us to be together. In his usual quiet way Mike let me babble on and on, and then he replied, "Me, too." Once I calmed down we formed a plan for my return. I couldn't leave until the end of March when winter quarter ended. So there it was: a final decision. I would abort my dream of a degree midway. Love had taken over my very being, and I was powerless to stop it. Nor did I want to.

The magic in my life continued when my ex-husband sold our house. Not only would I receive some cash, but also the timing was perfect. Mike had insisted that my daughters live with us in Eureka so we could be together. Julie had graduated from high school in January and was thinking about college, and Cyndi was just happy to have me back in her life.

I got a ride out of Mexico with a friend who dropped me at Mike's parents' in Huntington Beach, California. The three of us had met a few months earlier during Christmas in Eureka. David and Peggy were thrilled to see me again because they adored their son and were relieved that at age thirty-two he had finally found his perfect other half. They drove me to the airport and I flew off to the next chapter of my life.

Charlotte Plantz

My old house had to be vacated within the week, so there was no time to lose. Fabian refused to help us load furniture into a U-Haul truck. In fact, he stood drinking beer and watching as a crew of teenagers and I hauled out room after room of household items. Julie's boyfriend at the time volunteered to drive the U-Haul to Eureka, a trip of three hundred miles begun in pouring rain. Our little group arrived with Julie's black Lab at our new home that Mike had rented on April Fools' Day-in pouring rain. It didn't stop raining until June.

The three-bedroom frame house sat on the median strip between two one-way streets that actually are U.S. Highway 101, which runs through Eureka. A Poodle Parlor was on the south side of our house, and a Quik Loan office on the north side. A Red Lion Inn was directly across the street so at night the area was bathed in red neon. As soon as we were settled, Mike's friend Larry Sanborn began to show up on a regular basis. Larry was younger than Mike, but like our friend, Murray, Larry was wise beyond his age, and he also had an air of otherworldliness about him. The longer we knew Larry, the more that became apparent.

Many times during dinner I had the sense that Larry was about to show up, and within minutes he was at our door. During one of those dinners Mike made the connection to Julie being the blond girl he had met at his parents' house three years earlier when she was with Barry and the Blackfeet Indian kids, camping in the back yard. Until that moment, Julie had not made the connection either.

Larry had no car so he traveled around the city on his bicycle. When he graduated from high school he had hired on at Simpson Timber, where his father was about to retire. Larry's mother had always been a homemaker.

152

Me and My Magical Life

The boy was their only child, and he had been born late in their marriage. He grew to speak a language his family would never understand, but they loved one another unconditionally.

Mike and I became Larry's surrogate family because we happened to speak his language. It was a language of art, literature, philosophy, and magical realism. Mike and Larry played "mind" tennis that I once watched in slow motion as the two of them read each other's moves. It was an uncanny experience. Another one occurred when Mike took me backpacking in the Trinity Alps. We were on a trail about five miles in when we realized Mike had forgotten a second cup and I had forgotten ChapStick. We had stopped at a spring for a drink, and my lips were parched as we shared the one tin cup.

The two of us were sitting on a log when Larry appeared from around a bend with his arm extended. Mike and I were stunned when Larry said, "Hi, I thought you might need these," and handed us a tin cup and a ChapStick. We hadn't seen him in several weeks so we were astonished but on some level not surprised, for by then we had witnessed several otherworldly feats by Larry. Our young friend was a passionate and inventive artist who never stopped pushing boundaries.

Larry was a gifted photographer who later caught the eye of the Dalai Lama when they met in Bhutan, thanks to a Bhutanese tennis student. For three years Larry was the Dalai Lama's personal photographer. And then he slipped back into his old life in Eureka as though it never happened. Nothing Larry ever did was a big deal to him; he just kept making art. He owned an indoor tennis club and lived on-site in a little apartment. He gave lessons and created computer-generated kaleidoscopic art that once appeared on the side of a forty-story building in New York City during an international art show. We have a collection of Larry's Dalai Lama photographic art from that period and for forty years have been the recipients of Larry's stunning creativity.

Mike had his job at the lumber mill, but I couldn't find work of any kind. Given my energy level that was not a good thing, especially after my exhilarating teaching life in Mexico. We did a lot of hiking and beach combing on the weekends, but the in-between days took a toll on us females. Julie decided to move to Santa Cruz and enroll at San Jose State University for a nursing degree. About the same time, Cyndi decided to move to Minnesota to be near her dad and elderly grandparents. Mike looked at our family situation and within a short time came up with a solution.

With Julie and Cyndi moving on, Mike proposed that the two of us go to San Miguel de Allende so I could finish my degree. He said he had saved a thousand dollars to get us there and thought the school might be willing to rehire me. I was instantly taken with the idea and phoned the school the next day. To my relief and delight, not only was I hired on the spot, I was assured they were thrilled to have me back.

Once my teaching job was assured, we had to disassemble our household. The girls departed, and Mike and I found places for our furniture. Mike's sister, Sue, had a large house that would accommodate most of our belongings. She and Dale were gracious and generous in their offerings. They were so happy for Mike and his newfound happiness they would have done anything to help. By the beginning of August, Mike and I were on the road in his old Nash Rambler, down Highway 101 to his parents' house in Huntington Beach. Mike would leave the car with them.

Me and My Magical Life

David and Peggy drove us to the airport. Mike's mother wept from happiness for her son. She said she had always thought of Mike as an artist and was thrilled to have him heading to an art institute-even if it was in Mexico. My friend Rodda's mother was living with her for a while in their Aldama house, and they invited us to stay with them while we looked for a rental. Mike and I found a lovely little house on a quiet street near the Instituto that had everything we needed. It was next door to an Australian wild woman who was a weaving teacher at the school.

Gretchen Granger had been teaching weaving in the Highlands of New Guinea until her contract ran out. She and her daughter, Morley, had recently arrived in Mexico and were anxious to make friends. That act happened quickly in a place like San Miguel. People from all over the world came and went frequently, so bonds were formed almost immediately. In an exotic setting, expats have to share the experience, even if it's brief. It's not a bad thing-the memories last forever.

Mike and I loved that little house. Every few days we heard Gretchen hollering for us over the high wall that separated our homes. Sometimes the woman would climb up a ladder and appear above us to invite us to a proper English tea or evening cocktail. She taught us to make yogurt and a simple cheese and never failed to make us laugh. It was good to be back in that wonderful little city.

Mike and I wound up living with Gretchen for two weeks when the owners of our little casita decided to return to San Miguel. Our move took place just before the end of the school quarter and our wedding. Gretchen's water heater, like many in town, was a terrifying thing to operate. It had to be lit every time it was used and then shut off. One time, we forgot to turn the water heater off in our little casita. In the middle of the night we were awakened by the sound of water running down the stairs from the roof. We jumped out of bed and Mike ran to turn off the gas, but not before we saw boiling water spewing out of the relief valve on the roof. Gretchen had given us a stern warning about not touching her beast. She was the only one who had the knack for lighting it without incident. If not done just right, there could be a minor explosion.

One late afternoon, Mike came home from his pottery class covered with clay. Gretchen was teaching and wouldn't be home for several hours. Mike paced back and forth for a while and then declared, "I don't care what Gretchen says, I am going to light the water heater. I have to have a shower." I stood back while he put a match to the pilot, and almost immediately there was a loud whoosh as it exploded.

Mike was wearing a T-shirt and the flames singed all the hair on his arms. He did not get a shower until Gretchen showed up. And we never told her about the fireball. Mike had to wear long-sleeve shirts until we moved to the apartment behind the bullring. When we eventually moved into Rodda's house, we were relieved to find an on-demand water heater with a continuous pilot light, so we never had to worry about explosive bathing rituals.

17
The Wedding

We still laugh about it today: bullfight music as it bounced off the walls of the upstairs apartment. Mike and I were gathering our nuptial attire for the approaching ceremony down the hill at Judy Roberts's compound. Mike was especially sensitive to the moment. He just hoped the music wasn't a harbinger. He thought significant music on your wedding day held special meaning. I am much more practical on such matters. Since we lived on a hill behind the bullfight ring, and it was approaching noon on a Saturday, the music neither surprised nor intimidated me, although I did find it amusing.

It was disturbing though when I looked out the bedroom window to see a cart, being pulled by a tractor, holding the carcass of a newly vanquished *toro*. Good day for the *matador*, bad day for the bull, and how about for a wedding? The impending ceremony had not even been our idea. As the trumpets continued to blare, we asked one another, "How did this happen? Do you remember talking about a wedding?" The answer to that question is how our marriage came about.

On a late afternoon in early November, Judy Roberts, Natasha Bartachi, and I were sitting in the little Instituto book store/coffee shop taking a break between the classes we were all teaching: Judy taught weaving,

Natasha jewelry, and I taught the fabric printing class. I'm still not sure how the subject of marriage came up, but that was the topic of the moment between the three of us. Natasha remarked that Mike and I seemed so perfectly suited for one another, and then Judy asked whether Mike and I ever talked about getting married. I replied we hadn't even given it a thought. It was the seventies and hip to think of institutions as unimportant.

I could tell Natasha was in a romantic mood. She was involved in a relationship that was complex, to say the least. Natasha's paramour was married and lived in Arizona, but traveled on business to Mexico. He and Natasha would usually meet in Puerto Vallarta, which required considerable effort on Natasha's part since Puerto Vallarta is on the west coast, and we were in the middle of the country. Mike and I were the phone connection between the two lovers because the scorned Arizona wife had a private detective on her errant husband's tail.

The affair ended when the enraged wife ran over her husband in Arizona-and killed him. But at the time of our coffee klatch, Natasha was madly, passionately in love. Possibly because of the marriage situation with her lover she turned her fantasy toward me. Out of the blue, my friend exclaimed, "You and Mike have to get married. Here in San Miguel de Allende. Before we leave for winter break." The ball was already rolling, and I guess I didn't want it to stop.

Judy jumped in to say we should have the ceremony at her house because there was an old crumbling chapel at the back of the courtyard. She had plenty of room for lots of people. The plan escalated from there. I roared with laughter when Natasha said the wedding should be held on November 17 because the

Me and My Magical Life

Qantas Airline crew would be flying into Mexico City from Australia. They were friends of Natasha and Judy and loved a good party so they would be happy to provide the booze. School let out on November 16, so everyone could be there for the celebration. Mike and I had planned to leave for the States a few days later, so we would turn that into a honeymoon.

News traveled fast around the Instituto. By the next morning when I stopped by the office on my way to class, Norma, the office manager, told me she would like to bake the wedding cake. Before the day was over, others on staff had offered tokens of food, champagne, toasting goblets, a silver service, and even someone to perform the ceremony. An American studying jewelry was an official in the Baha'i faith and heard about the wedding plan. He came to me, offering to perform the ceremony. He was also a poet and said he would love to write the vows. Mike and I had never seen anything come together so fast.

Mike always came to my classroom at the end of the teaching day and we walked home together. Because we had our comida in the middle of the day, our evening routine was to put some snacks together and take them, with our drinks, up to the roof where we watched the sunset. That was also our time to share the day's events. The evening after my conversation with Judy and Natasha, I started to tell Mike about the wedding plan but he laughed so hard that I was momentarily horrified by the thought that maybe he never intended for us to be married.

Just before I went into shock, Mike, still laughing, said, "You won't believe what I'm about to tell you. It happened today in my Spanish class." He told me he was approaching the door to the classroom when he noticed one of the students carrying a case of beer.

Other food items appeared as students filed in. Mike addressed the class, "All right. A party. What's the occasion?" The beer carrier replied, "It's your engagement party. It's a surprise party." Mike said he couldn't believe what he was hearing, but he got into the spirit of the event. Stifling a laugh, he looked at me and asked, "Is there something we need to talk about?"

Mike and I had talked about marriage in the past. But that was then, and here we were living in Mexico nearly a year later and the subject had just come up again. So I guess it was actually I who proposed. I had to ask Mike how he felt about having a real wedding in a foreign country. One of the reasons I have loved Mike so much is the fact that he has always been totally honest about everything in life. I knew I could trust him completely to tell me exactly what he was feeling.

I had to laugh when he told me how much he enjoyed being the center of attention at his engagement party. He said a warm feeling wrapped around him as the party progressed. Or I thought, " It could have been the beer in the middle of the afternoon." Mike chuckled when I shared that thought, then pulled me into his arms. He thought being married in San Miguel de Allende sounded really romantic and was the right thing to do.

Not more than two weeks passed from the afternoon in the coffee shop with my friends to the day of the ceremony. The Instituto was a small, insulated world, made more so by the fact that we were all expats, thrown together by whatever fateful events had sent us south of the border. Every day held some little surprise for us.

The Qantas crew had indeed agreed they must be part of the celebration. There was no question about them providing the liquor. We thought that was a huge contribution, especially since we had no extra money.

Me and My Magical Life

Judy, who besides teaching a weaving class had a fashion business that supported several local Mexican women, came up with a wedding dress that fit me perfectly. People stopped me every day to let me know they were taking care of some aspect of the wedding celebration.

It was a good thing this took place at the beginning of our time in San Miguel, because my class load grew to such an extent that the next two years would have been overwhelming having to fit a wedding into the picture. As planned, school ended on November 16, 1974. The next day, as trumpets sounded from the bullring, Mike and I set off down the hill, carrying all our wedding attire in plastic bolsa bags.

Judy's house was a buzz of activity. I could not believe how many people were there, putting the pieces together. The ceremony was planned for four o'clock, and as we changed into our wedding clothes, children began running around all over the place. Judy's son, Brent, was about ten years old, and Natasha' son, Jimmy, and his sister were eight and six. There were a few other children gathering, and I thought I saw balloons peeking out back behind the old chapel. All of a sudden the ceremony was upon us.

The poet stood in front of the altar with Mike to his left. The Qantas copilot walked me up the aisle. The poet read his poem, and Mike and I recited the vows that had been written for us. Mike gave a little speech about the joy of being married under such romantic circumstances. And then a big whoop went up as the children unleashed a slew of balloons that rose out of the courtyard into the evening sky.

The next instant, we heard music. The wide, old wooden gates of Judy's house swung open to reveal the entire group of twenty-two Estudiantina musicians

Charlotte Plantz

parading into her courtyard. They serenaded the bridal couple as they entered. I nearly swooned with delight, for I had been a "groupie" of theirs for the past year. Their presence was a wedding gift to us, and one the two of us have never forgotten. But we did chuckle when the group began a rousing rendition of Oh' Susanna for our wedding dance.

The Estudiantinas are groups of musicians that go back to the seventeenth century and the days of Spanish rule. The groups are found throughout Mexico and have become a source of national pride. They dress in seventeenth-century costumes: ruffled shirts, black knee pants with long white stockings, black patent leather shoes with big silver buckles, and best of all, flowing black capes lined with red satin. This group presented quite a spectacle, and all were extremely fine musicians. Before Mike joined me in Mexico, Rodda and I used to frequent all the nightclubs in San Miguel to hear the Estudiantinas play. A few times we rode back to town on their old bus after one of their performances. Wherever they played, you could be sure Rodda and I would be there.

Rodda had arranged the superb surprise, and the musicians were thrilled to be part of it. Suddenly, goblets and champagne appeared out of nowhere, and the party began in earnest. Mike got a little drunk and we danced our feet off the rest of the evening. We both agreed it was the best wedding we could ever have imagined, and all our friends felt the same.

Mike and I got a ride to Taos with an Instituto classmate and spent a few days with Murray and his new lady, Pat. They were living in a lovely adobe house on a ridge outside of Taos, overlooking a broad valley with a river running through it. We newlyweds spent our

Me and My Magical Life

honeymoon in a guest casita, where the door had to be propped up against the five-degree weather. We survived due to a pile of blankets on the bed. Murray gave us a ride to the airport in Albuquerque, and we were off to California to spend the next month with our families.

When we returned to San Miguel de Allende and the Instituto after Christmas, we had another surprise. Sterling Dickenson, the school president, and Bill Parker, the dean, called us into Sterling's office and told us to sit down. Sterling and Bill were like two little kids; the two of them were so excited to tell us that the Instituto Allende would give Mike free tuition as a wedding gift for as long as we were there. It was an incredibly generous gift, and a turning point in Mike's life. It was where he became an artist.

18
The Next Two Years

Once we returned to Mexico, the honeymoon was over, in every sense of the word. Rodda and Susan, her mother, wanted to return to Texas, so Susan asked us to move into their house in order to keep Antonia, the maid, and Luis, the gardener, so they would be available to them in the future. Our only expenses would be paying the help and the electric bill. The next two years were a blur as I hit the road, running from the moment we entered the arched opening of the Instituto. I carried eighteen units toward my degree and taught two three-hour classes a week. Had it not been for Antonia tending to our daily needs, there was no way I could have maintained such a schedule. Mike and I continued our daily Spanish classes and played as much tennis as possible to get the kinks out.

We rarely socialized because I was constantly studying for one exam or another or working on lesson plans for my teaching classes. For classes in art history and Mexican art history, I did sketches on 3x5 cards with descriptions on the back. During every meal I flipped through the cards several times until they became familiar. After final exams I was kept at the door to be informed that I had received honors in each of the classes. It would be years before I became aware that I have a bit of a photographic memory.

165

Charlotte Plantz

Mike had the time of his life exploring every art class the school offered. The newlywed was an immediate natural at pottery. The students mined the clay and processed it for use on kick wheels that were set up outdoors under a *portal*. Great being outdoors, except for occasional buzzing bees and in summer, mosquitoes. The first piece Mike threw was a coffee pot, followed by eight cups of various sizes. The teacher, Roger Gregory, couldn't believe what he saw and not knowing how to relate to his new student, he simply ignored Mike.

Roger Gregory returned to Florida, but there were other pottery teachers along the way who inspired Mike. Two years later, as we were packing up to leave, Roger came back and asked Mike to show him his pots. He also wanted to apologize for ignoring Mike. He said he had never had a student with such natural talent and he hadn't known what to say for fear he would jinx it. Roger was thrilled to see what his former student had accomplished and encouraged him to continue throwing pots.

A highlight for us during our time in San Miguel was a Friday ritual that we continued to the end. I had produced a lot of hand-dyed, painted fabric that a wonderful family of seamstresses sewed into clothing. Their young daughters did a lot of embroidery for me as well. I sold designer clothing to tourists during crafts fairs at the school, giving us another source of income.

The sewing family lived in a large compound in a *barrio* about a half-mile from the school. Every Friday Mike and I walked or drove to the compound with bags of fabric. Three families lived in the compound: the *señor* and *señora* and their two sons, who were stone carvers, and their families. Their wives and daughters kept busy with my textile requests.

Me and My Magical Life

Our Friday ritual began as a request by the *señora*, who asked if we knew how to make biscuits: the American kind. She said they were too expensive to buy for their large family. And then she mentioned pancakes that were sold as a mix in boxes that were out of their price range. Mike and I offered to give a demonstration the following Friday on the fine art of biscuit making. The *señora* assured us they would have the ingredients ready. The kitchen in the compound was a large, square room with three new stoves with glass oven doors lining one wall. Each family had their own refrigerator in a line on an opposite wall. The kitchen floor was packed earth and water was dipped out of a huge clay container in a corner.

A screened door opened into the stone-carving yard, where the men were at work. The soapstone artists carved everything from ashtrays to large fountains, and they were fine craftsmen. Another door opened into the living room, where young girls sat embroidering. Thus everyone in the compound was privy to the conversations in the kitchen.

That first Friday cooking class was a delight, as each woman knelt in front of her oven window, watching biscuits rise. A lot of giggling and banter took place as we waited for the biscuits to come out of the oven. One by one, the men moved toward the back door as the aroma wrapped around them. The children gathered at the other door in anticipation. Fortunately, there were enough biscuits to go around, and it became a joyous event. The next demonstration was even better: Mike had the three women up to their elbows in pancake batter.

When it was time to cook on their individual griddles, the women squealed in delight as Mike helped them flip the pancakes. They had been terrified of that simple act and were relieved by how easy it was. By the time it was over, the women thought they had conquered the world. Once again all the other family members gathered by the doors waiting for the Friday treat.

After that event we began trading cooking demonstrations. Mike and I offered an American dish or product. And the following week, the family showed us a Mexican dish of our choice. That led to *ronpope*. I had always wanted to try making it but felt intimidated. I found a recipe and the *señora* instructed us to buy a liter of pure grain alcohol at a *farmacia* for the following week.

Ronpope requires a lot of egg yolks, sugar, and milk. The eggs are beaten to a "rope" stage. Sugar is added and then, slowly, the milk. It is cooked until it begins to thicken, and then the alcohol is trickled in. Mike kept stirring and gradually adding alcohol. He looked at the *señora* for a sign when to stop. But she kept saying, "*Un poco mas. Un poco mas.*" The men, huddled by the door, started to laugh at the amount of alcohol being added.

Mike and I took one liter of *ronpope* and left the rest for the family. We put the jar in the fridge on the patio and told Antonia not to touch it because it was so potent. She informed us that she did not drink alcohol, "So not to worry." The following day, Mike and I came home from school at 6:15 p.m. and found Antonia drunk out of her mind. She was giggling as she told us she just had to have a taste, and then couldn't stop because it was so good. The two of us had to hold Antonia up and walk her over a mile to her home. She would never have agreed to sleep it off at her employer's house.

Before we left San Miguel, our Friday friends had a big party for us. They cooked all the food and the men serenaded us with guitar music. Mike and I were each

Me and My Magical Life

presented with an embroidered shirt, and by then, we all had tears in our eyes.

One of my favorite memories is of the *señora* on a day when Mike was ill. When I arrived alone, she asked, *"¿Donde esta Miguel?"* After I told her he was sick, she said, "Well, I'd rather not do it today. He's the one I like to gossip with." I'm sure that Mike was the only man to be welcome in the *señora's* kitchen.

When my final quarter was drawing to a close, I was called into the office and reminded that in order to graduate I had to take the English ACT exam. I had foolishly chosen to push that toward the end because of my overloaded schedule. I had two weeks to cram for the test. All I could do at that point was check out a college freshman English textbook from the library and make notes on my trusty 3x5 flash cards. I simply added them to the pile left permanently on the dining room table. I had always been a slow eater and that worked to my advantage, as I flipped through the cards, chewing methodically, at every meal. Mike and I were playing tennis when someone from the office came rushing toward us, shouting the news, "Charlotte, you aced the ACT." I was about to become a graduate of the Instituto Allende.

The final quarter ended with me taking to my bed for two solid weeks. I could not speak. My legs wouldn't hold me up and I cried a lot. Mike and Antonia took care of all my needs while I slept for hours. My brain had simply stopped working. By the second week, I asked Mike to give Antonia a week's paid vacation so I could be free of her constantly checking in on me. You have to understand that was no small request because Antonia's job was her refuge. At home she shared a bed with three siblings. Seventeen other relatives kept the compound lively and generally in chaos.

Charlotte Plantz

At our house she had color TV and a daily routine that involved a trip to the *mercado*, with friends along the way for gossip. And she had a crush on Mike. Antonia's idea of a vacation was her job. Poor Mike, he spent an hour pleading with her to give us a one-week vacation to help me recover. He came into the bedroom with sweat streaming down his face. My exhausted spouse whispered, "I got three days. That's it." I recovered in spite of Antonia. When it was time for us to leave, she begged us to take her along. How we would have loved to do that. The three of us had become like family.

If Mike and I had any doubts about leaving our fairytale life, an event took place that made Mike sick to his stomach. He was at the mercado and witnessed a group of young boys playing "kick the rat." The outdoor market was infested with huge rats. On the way home, Mike noticed an old woman sitting on the side of the road. She and a dog were fighting over a bone. Mike was shaking as he entered the house and blurted out, "I can no longer take the poverty and brutality of life here. It's time to go." Within hours, we got a phone call from a local friend whose father worked on Wall Street. He told her to warn her friends to get their money out of *pesos* because the *peso* was about to devalue. Mike and I had around $2,000 US in *pesos* at the bank. We quickly withdrew it in dollars. Within two days the *peso* dropped dramatically, and we would have been wiped out. It was a dramatic end to a dream life.

With the old blue Dodge packed to the roof, Mike and I set off for our next adventure. Our destination was Chacon, New Mexico, where we had met four years earlier. It was June, the same month the two of us had arrived in Chacon that earlier summer. We were able to rent an old adobe house for $75 a month. It had no running water. No bathroom. Cooking had to be done on a wood cookstove-in the heat of summer. None of that fazed us; we were just happy to be back in that beautiful valley. We had our savings and thought we might be able to put some kind of creative business together that would support us. That turned out to be a premature idea, but we forged ahead.

Our little house was not near the river so we had to come up with a bathing solution. We found an old galvanized washtub and hauled it out next to the acequia, where water ran through the little ditch to irrigate fields. Mike filled the tub using a bucket and then covered the tub with black plastic. He did the preparation in the morning so the plastic would have time to heat the water. Shortly after lunch, before the monsoon rain moved in, we were able to take a hot bath. It worked perfectly unless there was too much cloud cover. We planted a little garden of lettuce and a few vegetables, all the while trying to come up with creative ventures that would support us.

Murray was living in Taos, so he came over on a regular basis. For my birthday he brought John Nichols's new novel, The Milagro Beanfield War. I never laughed so hard at a book. His characters were hilarious, and at the same time, profound and wiser than most. The setting was similar to where we were living at that moment. As it turned out, more than forty years later I published a book with characters in a similar setting, one hundred miles south of the milagro beanfield.

My birthday falls on July 21 and on that day I wanted to do something special, so Mike and Murray planned to take me to dinner in Mora. Just as we were getting ready to leave we heard what sounded like a freight train roaring toward us. We ran outside and stopped in our tracks as we saw a wall of hail headed up the valley, and it was a monster.

Charlotte Plantz

We ran around picking up anything not nailed down and tried to cover the little garden, but it was too late. We ran for the house as Murray picked up a Mexican beer tray and held it over his head so he could get to his truck and roll the windows up. The roar was so loud we couldn't hear one another, especially as it pounded the tin roof. When the storm was over, we found our bathtub plastic cover in shreds, and the little garden had been obliterated.

As we stood looking at the destruction, Mike and I were shocked into reality. We were in the wrong place at the wrong time. How could we survive the winter? And we had yet to come up with a business plan to support us. Mike said wistfully, "It's time to get real and head to California and the lumber mill. I know I can get a job there."

The next day we called Julie in Santa Cruz to tell her of our plan. She said she was ready to leave her life there and would fly out to drive back with us. Meanwhile, I found a huge supply of fabrics at a going out of business sale. I bought rayon, cottons, and white cotton velvet yardage for 25 cents and 50 cents a yard. There was so much fabric we had to rent a small U-Haul trailer, but I knew it was the beginning of a new venture for my creative juices.

It was great having Julie with us again, and as always, another adventure. By the time we got on the road Julie decided she wanted to return to Santa Cruz and start nursing school, so that was our first destination. Mike and I split our money with Julie, she moved in with a friend, and we were off to Eureka and Simpson Timber Company.

Mike was right; he got hired right away. The lumber mills were always looking for good workers. His artistic career had to be put on hold for a while, and it wouldn't be long before my own creative path was diverted. But not before I experienced a burst of creative energy-in spite of the incessant rain. We moved into a small one-bedroom apartment in an old Victorian house, but I found ways to paint fabrics in spite of the cramped quarters.

I actually came up with a technique that embraced the rain: it involved sprinkling powdered Procion dyes on lengths of fabric that were lying on the ground. I had to work fast, using an umbrella until the dye had been dispersed. Then I stepped onto the porch and watched the rain create patterns as it hit the fabric. Designs were created by the intensity of the raindrops. A lot of clothing came together out of our brief stay in that apartment, but I longed for a studio and more space. Fortunately, that happened soon.

19
422 Second Street

A few years ago a friend sent me a newspaper article about Old Town Eureka, specifically Two Street, as it was called back before the days of redevelopment. The street was one of several blocks of the fishing industry waterfront on Humboldt Bay. It was a wild and woolly place up until the mid-seventies, when Mike and I moved there. According to our landlord, Norton Steenfott, who had driven a cab in Old Town during its heyday of wildness, on any given Saturday night the police closed Two Street. They set up blockades that kept everyone inside from leaving and everyone outside from entering. The police allowed those inside the blockade to whoop and holler-and work it out among themselves-and then they drove off in their patrol cars down a side street.

      Loggers and fishermen had a reputation as some of the toughest characters on the planet due to their vocations. Danger had always been an intrinsic part of their jobs, and the need to let off steam at that time ran in the same channels. No self-respecting Eurekan would be caught dead venturing into that neighborhood at night. There was little beyond empty buildings with boarded-up windows facing the street; saloons and brothels catered to the only needs the revelers had on weekend nights. According to Norton, fist fighting could take place indoors or out, depending on the weather.

Charlotte Plantz

Mike and I were introduced to the Old Town neighborhood by a new acquaintance of mine. Ann Mendenhal had lived on Two Street for over twenty years and knew the place intimately. We had recently met as students in the home health aide program sponsored by the Humboldt Senior Resource Center. One day during a break, Ann and I were talking about life and what we were doing in a home health aide program. I told Ann about living in small quarters and trying to create and ended by saying how much I would give to live in a place with a big bathtub, cheap rent, and creative space. I asked her if she knew of such a place.

Ann told me she supported herself writing pulp fiction and could relate to the need for creative space. She pondered my question and then said she knew of a place. But it would take an open mind and a lot of work to make it "homey." Our new friend added that she had a lot of surplus "stuff" to help in the transition. I told her I would talk to Mike and let her know the next day whether we would like to look at it. After living in Chacon, New Mexico, and buying a one-way ticket to Mexico, living on Two Street did not seem too daunting. Mike agreed that evening and the next day Ann and I made a date to look at the flat.

It was January 1977, a bitter cold, foggy evening when Ann unlocked the front door at 422 Second Street. She led us up a wide, long staircase to the landing of the flat, where a pay phone still hung on the wall. My eyes were pulled up over the doorway to where an exit sign glowed bright red. Down at the end of the five-foot-wide hallway, a second red exit light cast an eerie glow over the back door, which was about fifty feet from where we stood. Mike and I were scarcely breathing. We held hands clenched together like knots, unable to move until Ann began turning on lights in rooms that opened onto the long hall. We laughed nervously as we began moving down the hall.

The building had once been used for office space over a store or business of some kind on the street level. The area now referred to as Old Town went back to the eighteen hundreds and had only recently been renovated. All the storefronts had been painted in Victorian colors, though there were not many businesses at the time we moved there. 422 was also home to Angelus Clockwork Music Store on the street level, one of two businesses on the block. The building had been painted in three colors, pink, rose, and lavender, while the building to the right wore yellow, mustard, and green, and so on down the block. Back upstairs, Ann excitedly pointed out the potential of various rooms, offering free paint, ladders, curtain material, and a variety of wallpaper.

She sounded like a car saleswoman, upbeat and positive, as she sought to have us enter her world of possibilities. For as it turned out, Ann and Norton were playing the role of boosters for the neighborhood they so dearly loved. The two of them hoped to entice creative people to move into the area because that would add "flavor" to the redevelopment project. Mike and I seemed to have the necessary ingredients, for we were being noticeably wooed.

In spite of the damp cold and gloomy atmosphere, Mike and I began to notice details in the huge flat. There were twelve rooms, counting the pantry off the kitchen, where the sink was located. The pantry had a long counter with open shelves above and cabinets below and a small window up high, near the ceiling. Except for two large rooms at the front that looked out on a plaza across the street and two rooms at the other end, all of the other rooms opened onto the long hallway. Twenty feet above the hall, a skylight ran the length of the hall. As it turned out, the skylight was probably the only reason we wound up living there for seven years. We must have had one of the few places in Humboldt County that did not reek of musty mold.

At one time each room had had windows facing the hall, but when it was turned into a brothel, the windows had been replaced with drywall. That would have been daunting because there were no other windows; the rooms were like caves. One morning when I was in my studio with a window open to the plaza, I heard two men on a bench talking about the good old days at 422, when our home had been a house of ill repute.

The next thing we noticed was the furniture that had been shoved together in the living room. It was apparent that all the pieces had recently been reupholstered-in an array of garish fabrics. When I mentioned that to Ann, she laughed and replied that she had done it. She told us that she lived in the small office building of what had been her late husband's trucking business, two blocks west of 422. She had a lot of storage space, so all sorts of businesses in Eureka donated things to Ann, things like paint, wallpaper, fabrics, etc., etc. They knew she would find ways of either putting to use or dispensing to others the goods that were outdated or out of style. It was a practice Mike and I have always approved of in our own life. We were the perfect match-up.

As Mike and I went from room to room, we saw graffiti along the hallway. "Fuck you, Norton" had been scrawled on both sides, along with "Free the cockroaches, they have a right to live." In the kitchen, small holes were punched in the walls and the same cockroach slogans scribbled alongside the holes. Ann pointed out that junkies had been living upstairs. Then we saw a car engine in one of the back rooms, along with several syringes strewn about. Mike and I shuddered and squeezed our knotted hands even tighter. But by then, we knew we were going to live in that former brothel-junkie haven. The six-foot-long claw-foot bathtub had cinched it.

We told Ann to let Norton know we were interested, and then we remembered to ask what he wanted for rent. Her reply was, "Two hundred twenty-five dollars a month, and Norton doesn't want a lease. That's in case we're not compatible." Ann said Norton didn't own the building, but took care of it for an old friend. We asked her to arrange a meeting with our soon-to-be landlord and headed down the long stairway, out into the foggy winter night. We were astounded by our decision to take on such a massive project. We were also excited by the potential because it was a blank canvas-waiting for creative folks to show up.

We said goodbye to Ann as she headed into the thick mist toward her trucking compound. We could see that she was totally unafraid, completely comfortable in her surroundings, and that gave us comfort. Mike and I stood on the sidewalk for a while, taking in the scene. Rows of old-fashioned streetlights lined both sides of the street and the plaza facing us. In the center of the plaza a beautiful Victorian gazebo was perched atop a round brick platform. A graceful curved brick ramp with wrought iron railings led to the gazebo platform. The inside curve formed the wall of a fountain that flowed down and across the front of the gazebo base.

In the glow of soft yellow light diffused by fog, the entire plaza took on a surreal appearance, and we were heartened that it was completely deserted, with not a soul to be seen for several blocks in each direction.

We liked the fact that we were breaking into new territory by being among the first to live in the redevelopment neighborhood. While we stood in the muted silence, it slowly dawned on us that we would have to park our car in a parking lot on the next street and walk through the lovely plaza to reach our new home. That meant carrying groceries through the rain. Mike and I looked at one another without speaking, pondering another inconvenience. By mutual consensus we knew it was but a minor nuisance. We had already moved into the adventure.

Mike and I met with Norton the next day and knew immediately that our new landlord was a real character. Norton was in his sixties. He was not tall and was squarely built on short, beefy legs. I noticed his hands immediately; they were huge, with fat fingers, most of which were scarred and gnarly. He wore a dirty white painter's cap, a tattered, long-sleeve plaid flannel shirt and trousers that were held up by a too-long belt that hung down in front beneath his huge stomach. He had a nose like W.C. Fields's, large and slightly red, situated squarely in the middle of his huge head. He also had a twinkle in his eyes and a wry sense of humor. We liked him right off. Norton was a very up-front guy.

We learned over the years that our landlord said whatever was on his mind. If you had to fight with him once in a while because of his narrow view of life that was OK with him. Norton loved teaching things to people. If you were a quick learner, you had his respect forever. But if you didn't catch on, he never forgave you. Norton still related to you, but he looked down when he talked to you. That didn't happen with us, but I saw it on several occasions with young people he hired as helpers.

Me and My Magical Life

Our meeting with Norton took place on an especially cold, gloomy, gray day in front of the door to the flat. For the second time in two days we climbed the stairs to that unholy place. Norton took us through the flat, ignoring the graffiti, and in a steady stream of instructions, gave us the lay of the land, so to speak. He said all the furniture had to remain, because Ann had worked so hard to spruce it up. Shockingly, that included the beds. Who had occupied those beds? Oh boy!

We could paint the walls any color we wanted or wallpaper them if we liked. But we "Could Not Get Rid Of" the rubber tree that grew out of a chartreuse-colored, five-gallon paint bucket. The tree reached the skylight twenty feet above us, and was spindly-and ugly. Oddly, we had a good laugh over the fact that we couldn't throw it out. Norton said the kitchen stove could be cleaned at Ann's because she had a steam engine cleaner that her husband had used on his trucks.

Our landlord said he would bring carpet for the long staircase, but we would have to lay it. When I protested that I didn't know anything about laying carpet, Norton informed me that he would bring tacks and a hammer and give me a demonstration. He hoped we liked old rose, because the carpet was coming out of a church. He assured me that he would pick the cleanest part. I wound up rolling the carpet out at Ann's truck center and dying it red, using a paint roller and Procion dye that I had brought from Mexico. I did learn to lay carpet, although the result was slightly wavy, and Norton and I were both proud of my efforts.

All the walls in the flat had been painted grayish white years ago. A mass of wood trim around windows and doors had been painted an especially nasty acid blue that made my teeth ache. After dark, when the red exit signs were lit, the whole place took on a ghoulish cast that made us shudder. It was imperative that we start painting as soon as possible.

Mike and I nearly wore ourselves out cleaning the place before we could ever get to the painting. We steam cleaned the faded hall carpet and any furniture that had not been reupholstered. Then we tackled the mattresses. Those we actually steam cleaned a number of times and then covered with protective mattress covers. When Mike pulled the kitchen stove out to clean beneath it, he found a mound of grease that had run down for who knows how long. The pile was about six inches high because someone had removed the little grease-catcher pan; no wonder there were cockroaches. Norton did fill the holes in the kitchen walls. By the time we moved in, he had the engine removed as well as the syringes.

And then we tackled the painting, which continued for over a year. In addition to the twenty-foot-high walls in the hall, the staircase had some spaces that reached twenty-eight feet. All the remaining walls were fourteen feet high-and there were twelve rooms! Ann and Norton had helpers haul in scaffolding, immense ladders, and incredibly long paint rollers. Deliveries continued as they brought gallons and gallons of paint. Now and then we talked someone into helping us paint, but for the most part we did it ourselves.

We had three bedrooms, because we had three beds. We chose one room for storage and another as a formal dining room, even though it was fifty feet to the other end of the hall from where the kitchen was. A large room facing the plaza with windows ten feet tall became the living room. The room next to it, a bit smaller, was to become my studio. Two of the bedrooms were double rooms, so we used one as a sitting room in each set.

Me and My Magical Life

The room we used as our suite faced the back, where you could see a smaller brick plaza on the corner. The kitchen had two huge, tall windows that looked out on a small, two-story building across from us that faced the alley.

A long, creaky stairway led down along the brick wall to a little tunnel with a heavy wood door that opened to the alley. We had to carry our garbage out that way to the dumpster next to Norton's storeroom. One night I started down the stairs to take trash to the dumpster when I heard a strange noise. Something didn't feel right so I decided to wait. The next morning when I went down, Norton was sitting on a step next to the dumpster. He barked, "Hey, you better watch what you're throwing in the trash. You almost got me killed last night."

I nearly fell over as my mind flashed back to the noise I had heard the night before, and I told him, but Norton went on, "You always put your garbage in a brown bread bag, right?" I nodded, and he said the noise I had heard was from him. He was being beaten by two guys who were rummaging in the dumpster. Coming out of his storeroom, he had surprised them and yelled at them. One of the vagrants pulled out my brown bread bag, which had a big ham bone in it, and began hitting Norton on the head with it. Norton said he would have been a goner if old Bill hadn't come along and saved him.

Old Bill was close to ninety and owned a bar and poker room on Third Street at the end of the alley. He was closing up for the night and about to head home. The old man carried his daily receipts and a pile of cash in a bowling ball bag. He also carried a loaded gun. He used that to chase the vagrants away, saving his friend from more beating.

Norton had building supplies and all sorts of junk stored in most of the buildings along the alley. He owned some of the buildings and took care of others for old cronies of his. During the entire time we lived on Two Street we paid our rent to Norton, who was usually sitting on the lower steps of an upstairs apartment with an assortment of cats lined up on ascending stairs. At night, he went home to a house somewhere in town, but as far as we were concerned, he lived next door to us.

A young man named Martin Wong lived in the apartment above Norton's storeroom. He had recently graduated from Humboldt State University with a degree in fine arts and had a reputation as an incredible artist. We invited Martin to dinner one night, and he showed up barefoot, along with a Presbyterian minister and his wife. The five of us moved into the living room after dinner for conversation, and Martin began walking along the tops of the couches and chairs while we were sitting in them. It was a strange and interesting evening. At some point, Martin Wong asked if we would like to buy a piece of his art. We loved his work but didn't have much money so had to decline.

A few days after our dinner party, Martin approached us again. He needed money to get to New York and had a small painting that he wanted to sell us for twenty-five dollars. The artist showed us another intricate painting of his apartment for one hundred dollars, but we couldn't afford that, so we bought the cheaper painting. Had we known the future of the artist, we could have made the investment of a lifetime. Before his death, Martin Wong donated his huge collection of graffiti art to MOMA and had his own art featured in major collections.

There were three couches in the furniture pile, so we put the smallest in our sitting room at the back of the flat. The other two, huge overstuffed beasts, remained in the living room facing each other. The living room floor was covered with old, faded blue-flowered linoleum, and it had to go. We checked with Norton and he agreed, so we pulled it up and beneath it were layers and layers of newspapers used as padding. The entire tier was dated 1936, the year I was born. We took that as somehow synchronistic.

Beneath the papers were wide, worn wooden planks, a treasure find. There were two big, overstuffed chairs that remained in the living room. A red velvet chair went into the bedroom with my own old brass bed. That room always looked like it had been carried over from the brothel period. A senior craft woman eventually created a "hooker" doll with black fishnet stockings, and she sat in that red velvet chair the entire time we lived there.

We did have some of my old furniture that we added to the household, and then we began to frequent the St. Vincent de Paul store down on the corner of the next block. That store kept us entertained for years and became our Saturday morning ritual. Jim, the store manager, took a liking to us, and so did his employees, for we were an anomaly in the neighborhood. Mike and I were the only "regular" folks who lived in Old Town. There were hookers, winos, pimps, and drug addicts. Homeless men, called hoboes then, lived beneath unused railroad cars. Other than that, we were the first brave pioneers to settle into the area.

During our moving-in period, I was walking through the plaza carrying a bag of groceries when a guy sitting on one of the benches hollered at me. "Hey lady," he called. "Can I ask a favor?" He was obviously one of the serious drinkers, but I strolled over and stood in front of him. He asked for a cigarette, and I explained that I rolled my own and would be happy to give him paper and tobacco. He looked at me in deep thought for a moment and then held up his hands.

Every finger was wrapped in a Band-Aid. He said apologetically, "I can't do it." I placed my bag on the bench and sat down next to him. I fished around in my purse for my tobacco pouch and proceeded to roll the guy several cigarettes. I noticed he was grinning, impressed by my skill. As I handed him the smokes, he looked me in the eyes and asked, "What the hell are you doing down here?" I replied that we had just moved into 422 and were happy to be in the neighborhood. He held my gaze for a moment, then smiled and thanked me for the cigarettes.

The man never asked me for another thing after that, but we always smiled or nodded. The word went out that we were new in the area, but we were OK. Not one person ever bothered us the entire time we lived there, even though we always acknowledged each other's presence. Often, when Mike came home from work at the mill, usually driving slowly, for that was his way, there would be a hooker or two standing on the corner, beckoning to him. All of them laughed together. When we started roller-skating on the sidewalks of Old Town, invariably small groups of hookers were sitting on brick planters at the corner of Third and F. They were just hanging out in the rare sun or hustling their wares. But they always called out to Mike, who, according to Norton, skated like a bird flapping its wings. "Be careful honey, don't break that little tush."

Early in our time on Two Street, the police department sent two walking policemen to patrol the area day and night. One of their problems was keeping the hookers off street corners. Eventually the cops asked Norton for advice and were amused and grateful for his solution. The old man disappeared inside his storeroom and emerged with a long piece of metal with a handle on top. He led the cops to a planter in the plaza and stuck the metal rod into a faucet handle. Then he turned the sprinkler on high and sprayed the hookers sitting on the edge of a planter. The neighborhood laughed over that for years. And the hookers disappeared from street corners.

And then there was the mailman, who wore a rooster headdress on Halloween when he delivered the mail. And there was Marie, the wino lady who lifted her skirt and urinated off the edge of one of the lovely curved benches. Periodically a couple of police cars drove up on the plaza to corner Marie when she became especially rank. I could hear them holler from my open studio window, "Jeez Marie, you smell bad, let's take you in for a cleanup." They hauled her off to jail for a shower and a meal and then released her back to the neighborhood.

The only time I ever felt fear was a day when I was unlocking our door, and someone started shouting obscenities right behind me. I thought I was a goner until Norton happened by. He explained that the man suffered from Tourette's syndrome. For the umpteenth time I learned more about the human condition in that world previously unknown to me.

By the time we moved into the flat we had fallen in love with Old Town. The view out our front windows went beyond the lovely plaza to the bay another block beyond. A fishery warehouse blocked one corner of our view, but still gave us an expanse of water where we could see the Humboldt State crew racing teams skimming along the surface of the water in their shallow boats. They usually raced early in the morning, and with windows open you could hear voices shouting through their megaphones to "pull, pull." That was always a thrill. Especially when I realized they were out there in freezing drizzle most of the time.

Charlotte Plantz

The bay was lined with old warehouses, and a railroad track ran down the middle of First Street. Lazio's Seafood Restaurant sat on the wharf about two short blocks west of us. Fog's Fish and Chips was around the corner. Fog's served their fish and chips wrapped in newspaper and they were to die for. An Italian restaurant around another corner had a big side yard where they planted vegetables to be used in their dishes. They were way ahead of their time.

In some ways, Old Town reminded us of San Francisco on a very small scale. We walked everywhere and never tired of making new discoveries. One early Sunday morning in a drizzle, Mike and I walked along the railroad tracks that ran along the bay. We came to an empty space where the foundation of a house still remained. In front, next to where a door had been, was a big patch of Shasta daisies. We picked a huge bouquet, though the petals were covered with soot, which I intended to wash off when we got home.

We met Norton on our return trip and he took one look at the bouquet and remarked that we must have been down to Ma Green's place. I asked him how he knew that. The old man laughed as he replied, "Dirty daisies. It's the only place around where you'd find dirty daisies." Mike and I roared with laughter. It was on that walk that we heard hoboes talking beneath railroad cars.

For some time I had been writing a childhood friend about our new adventure. About a year after we moved in, Donna phoned to let us know that she, her husband, and parents wanted to visit. My friend's mom and dad, who lived in Los Angeles, had been surrogate parents to me as a girl so we were quite close. My friend lived in Sacramento, so this was a special trip for all of them. Mike and I were excited to have our first guests, especially because Mike's and my parents were horrified by what we were doing. They had no desire to visit their adult children in a former brothel.

The day Donna and family arrived, we gave them a tour of the flat and then gathered in the living room. There was a slight pause as we settled in, and then Donna said, "Charlotte, the four of us agree that your letters didn't even begin to exaggerate." By the time they left, they too had fallen in love with our place and the neighborhood.

20
My California Arts Council Career

When we arrived in Eureka with my new BFA degree, I was eager to get started in a new art-related career. I approached the directors of a new program for senior citizens. It was a pilot project for a government-sponsored approach to help create services for low-income elderly folks. My idea was to offer art and craft classes that would produce products that students could sell. The directors loved my idea, but my timing was off. Anne Weiss and Bev Jackson were busy trying to put the Senior Resource Center together, and their focus was on a home health aide program. Classes were about to begin, and the directors said if I was willing to enroll in the class they would help me write a grant proposal to the California Arts Council the following year. I enrolled in the class.

The home health aide class, a six-week course taught by a registered nurse and a social worker, covered basic health care skills to assist with personal grooming for housebound seniors, as well as social skills for folks who had become socially isolated. The most important thing I learned in that program was how creative retired folks had become, given the weather and time on their hands. Rain and overcast lasted most of the year so there was a lot of indoor activity. As I traveled around the county, I saw signs of creative hobbies by both husbands and wives. People pulled boxes of handwork from beneath their beds to share with me and I was stunned by the craftsmanship. My mind kept going back to the idea of producing crafts for sale through a senior cooperative craft store, but that didn't happen for a year or so.

Until then, I learned to bathe fragile bodies and do what I could to make people comfortable. Because I love people, it was a satisfying experience. I also learned about the aging process ... and death and dying. Elisabeth Kubler-Ross had recently come on the aging scene and I was fortunate to attend a couple of workshops with her. Kubler-Ross was well known for her work with the end of life process. Hospice grew out of that work and I felt lucky to be in such an enlightened environment. The first Alzheimer's Adult Day Care Center in the country began in Eureka. That opened a whole new world for me, and I found that knowledge helpful many years later when three close friends were diagnosed with Alzheimer's disease.

I was midway through the home health aide program when Mike suddenly required kidney surgery in San Francisco. Fortunately for us, Mike's brother, Bob, was living in the Castro District just a mile or so from UC Moffitt Hospital so I stayed with him. I spent a minimum of 12 hours a day with Mike, sometimes breaking it up so I could have dinner at home with Bob. That was until Mike suffered a serious setback that required another week's hospital stay. Another bed was put in Mike's room, and that's where I spent my time until his release. The staff felt Mike needed my energy to help with his healing, and they were right. It was a hip and enlightened teaching hospital, and we quickly learned just how advanced they were.

Me and My Magical Life

The patients in the kidney transplant ward had great freedom. If they were physically able, they could wander around visiting other patients. Some patients could have pizza, beer, and wine delivered if their doctor approved. One such patient was a happy-go-lucky guy named Antonio, who was across the hall from Mike's room. Antonio had severe diabetes and had lost both legs just below his hips. He was in the kidney ward because his kidneys were failing. And he was dying. But he didn't dwell on it. He had been in the ward for a while and knew his way around.

Antonio was a comedian and loved hosting pizza parties in his room for other patients. The party host moved around on a wheeled cart, zipping in and out of rooms, cheering people up. He dropped in one afternoon before I moved in to invite Mike to a party in his room that evening so he could introduce him to neighboring patients. Antonio paid for all the deliveries because, he said, "If I don't spend it now-when?" Mike didn't bother to ask his doctor for permission to drink a beer at that stage of his recovery. He just went and thought it a high point in his stay. As Mike pointed out, "The conversation at a party in the kidney transplant ward was guaranteed to be interesting." The nursing staff would agree.

The week I moved in with Mike, Antonio brought a teenage boy to meet us. Evan was in the hospital for the final of many surgeries on his penis. He was born with his penis on the inside, rather than the normal outside. For sixteen years his doctor had been performing surgeries trying to get the boy's body to something like normal. It had been a long and complicated procedure, and Evan's parents were adamant about the transformation even when their son begged to be left alone. The last surgery had been performed and Evan was waiting for the bandages to be removed. He walked around the ward and visited with other patients and began spending time in Mike's room.

During one of our visits, Evan told us that he was gay. Mike asked if he had ever considered transgender surgery. Evan said he had thought about that and decided to talk to his doctor about it. And then the bandages came off and poor Evan was devastated. The result was not anywhere near what he had hoped for. The boy spent a long time crying with us, so we decided to put him in touch with Bob, who was deeply involved in the gay rights movement in the city. Bob came to meet Evan and they had some good conversations, which Evan said helped him decide what to do. In the end, the boy decided to live with his body as it was, adding that it was too much to ask of his doctor to undo sixteen years of work.

At the end of the week, Evan came to our room with a young female friend. He wanted her to meet the man who gave good advice and his wife, who slept in a bed next to him. The four of us spent an hour together sipping juice and telling stories. Tina confessed that she was a "jumper." The young woman followed a goth subculture and loved jumping off bridges into water, but it got her in a lot of trouble with the law. Tina said her strange behavior resulted in being put on an alarm watch list. She was arrested several times in the act of jumping. She tried to assure us that her jumping had nothing to do with suicide, but that was hard to accept.

So that was our world for two weeks in San Francisco at Moffitt Hospital: a boy with a malformed penis and his "jumping" girlfriend. And the charismatic, legless diabetic who loved throwing pizza parties in his room. In the middle of our last week, I received a phone call from a home health client named Bert. I had been with

Me and My Magical Life

Bert on a weekly basis for several months and he was very attached to me. He was also a pain in the butt. The man had diabetes and was on oxygen. He chain-smoked while hanging over the bottom half of an outside Dutch door and dropping cigarette butts into a growing pile that I threw in the trash every week.

Bert did nothing for himself except complain. He called to tell me that if I didn't come home soon he was going to kill himself. By then, with our life full of tragic and courageous friends, I had become a bit delusional, living in a hospital room, breathing life into my husband. Even though it was not a home health aide thing to say, I told Bert, "Go for it."

I worked as a home health aide for over a year and then submitted my first grant request to the California Arts Council. The grant process was tedious and highly competitive so it took me a while to learn how to compress information in a compelling way. I had to capture the reviewer's attention and interest with as few words as possible. I had documented the vast array of handcrafts throughout the county. My proposal was to help elderly housebound folks find outlets for their handcrafted work that would generate a little income.

During that time, thanks to Governor Jerry Brown, there was a lot of interest in aging issues and the beginning of government-sponsored programs. My grant was accepted and I spent the next seven years fine-tuning creative projects for elders. I hired an assistant and had incredible luck when Jan Rader showed up to help implement programs. Jan was an inspired and patient teacher, and we worked together to the end of my time in Eureka and have remained friends.

Because I already had a connection with so many retired folks throughout the county, I began driving around and pitching my idea for a cooperative craft store. Every person I spoke to eagerly agreed to get on board, so I talked our landlord into renting us a cheap space for a store. It happened to be next door to where we lived, which turned out to be a good thing and a bad thing. The store was a democratic venture because all the members had a voice. They voted on everything, including the name: The Unique Boutique. There were over twenty members so there was plenty of stock for the store. I was surprised by the variety of work and especially how many men turned out with their woodwork projects.

Quilting was big in Humboldt County and handmade quilts became a big hit at the store. As word spread, buyers came from out of the area to stock up on Christmas gifts. A couple from Alaska came every year to buy quilts. I got a small grant to buy a sewing machine and fabric to make tote bags with a silk-screened picture of the store and surrounding gingerbread-trim buildings. We hand-painted the soft colors and then quilted the buildings. The bag became a moneymaker for the store.

That project spawned another involving stroke victims at Easter Seals (now called Easterseals). Jan and I had been teaching craft classes for clients when I got the idea for a small silk screen that could be operated by two stroke victims, each using one hand. My idea was to produce a product that could be sold, with proceeds going toward craft supplies. Mike worked out the silk-screen prototype and the two of us practiced using one hand until we had a smooth-running operation. Bonnie Kavanaugh, the Easter Seals director, loved our idea and we had no trouble signing up clients willing to give it a try. They began by producing silk-screened potholders with the Easter Seals logo and then on to tote bags.

Me and My Magical Life

With so many creative retired folks, senior centers sprang up in cities throughout the county, and I figured out ways to involve them in community projects. My friend Jane Hill, taught theater arts at College of the Redwoods, where I taught a craft class for a while. Jane's class produced at least one show a year and she had little money for costumes. I enlisted senior centers to help sew costumes, and for one show, knit stockings for the cast. In gratitude, Jane provided a bus to transport seniors to a free matinee performance.

I introduced health fairs, oral history projects, and public school mentoring volunteers. I talked some centers into sewing lap quilts to donate to local nursing homes and had school children deliver them. That was a big hit. We had a May Day flower basket project for housebound folks and whatever holiday-themed projects I could think up. For a long time I was free to generate as many creative projects as possible. And I just kept writing grant proposals that got accepted.

Mike and I had a friend named Anthony. He was a great musician, but his talent extended beyond his musical abilities, and those skills were directed toward disenfranchised people. Anthony was forever popping up in one nonprofit agency or another, always having to do with human services, and always with good ideas that would somehow benefit the recipients. One of his best ideas was one that I had wondered about myself, a collective consciousness sort of thing that happens all the time throughout the universe. Anthony came to me with his idea of a nursing home collective garden where residents could plant and grow vegetables, and then contribute produce to their own kitchens. I took the idea one step further, adding the concept of container gardens where residents who used wheelchairs could roll up to a planter and tend their plants.

Charlotte Plantz

In our wildest fantasies we had residents in the kitchens cleaning vegetables and contributing to the preparation of meals, something I am sure would horrify state nursing home regulators, but the thought gave us a warm glow. The problem for Anthony was that not one nonprofit agency would sponsor his ideas because of his unpredictability. He could not be trusted to write a grant proposal that would fund him money, even for the greatest idea in the world.

Poor Anthony. He came to me because he trusted me with his garden idea and asked that I write a grant proposal based on his concept, targeted specifically at residential nursing homes. I was more than ready for the task because I had already visualized the concept and knew exactly where to begin. My art programs had taken me to the local long-term care facilities, so I was known in that community.

When Bev Jackson read my grant proposal, she said she had tears in her eyes. She said, "No one would turn this grant down." And they didn't. And they gave me enough money to hire people and buy a few supplies. All of the lumber for planters was donated by a couple of redwood mills. The first person I hired was Anthony. Another was a Korean handyman named Kim, who was deaf and did not speak. Kim was a creative and innovative asset and we formed a special bond.

One day after the project finished I answered the doorbell to find my Korean friend standing next to his bicycle. Behind the seat he had tied a lovely little replica of a church with a spire that he had built using redwood scraps from our project. It was his gift to me, and the church was a replica of the church he attended. Both of us stood in silence as tears ran down our cheeks. And then we hugged and Kim rode off down Two Street. I never saw him again.

Me and My Magical Life

The wheelchair container gardens stirred up a lot of interest outside the area for a long time. Thirty-five years later my daughter Julie, worked as director of nursing in a new brain and spine rehab facility connected to Sutter Medical Center in Roseville, California. She had been with Sutter for years as surgical floor manager, so they asked her to be part of the design team for the new facility. Julie was involved with every aspect of the project and proposed adding a wheelchair container garden to the patio adjoining the common room. Everyone enthusiastically agreed. I was thrilled later to learn that patients were being allowed to work in the kitchen with the produce they picked. What an inspiration after all those years.

But we weren't finished with Anthony; he was usually at the edge of our life in some way. Anthony, the musician, had a girlfriend named Marilyn who sang the blues with so much feeling it made you ache to hear the words pouring out of her soul. Marilyn was African American and her music came out of her gospel music background, but life with Anthony provided the necessary pathos required for singing gut-wrenching blues. The gift of Anthony was that he could play piano to match Marilyn's voice even though he was white.

But Anthony suffered with the best of the great blues brothers, for he was plagued by serious bipolar disorder, which kept his life in a state of perpetual dysfunction. Anthony and Marilyn played and sang in clubs around the area, and it was always a joy to sit in the back of a dimly lit room, huddled with masses of people, usually college students from Humboldt State, all grooving on the music.

Except for once, when I arranged for Anthony and Marilyn to perform at a fundraising concert. The concert was held at the Humboldt Arts Center on First Street, one block from our flat. The night of the concert the place was sold out. And then Anthony and Marilyn showed up. Drunk. And Anthony had his right arm in a sling. My breath quickened and I knew we were in trouble. And I said so to the pair. Anthony sat down at the piano to show me that he could still play by leaning forward toward his right arm. He was such a good piano player he somehow made it work and I didn't know what else to do. So the show went on.

The couple started out well enough, but then Marilyn wandered around the room, microphone in hand. In a singsong voice, she ragged on Anthony, working herself into a frenzy. Soon she was swearing and begging the audience to take her side in whatever was going on between them. By then, Anthony, hanging over the keys, was singing, "Where is my singer? Where in the f--- is my singer?" And it went downhill from there. I couldn't breathe. And shame on me-I darted out the door and ran all the way home. To this day I don't know how that concert ended.

Twenty-three years later Mike and I learned that Anthony and others who suffered serious mental illness had been given a gift from a friend of ours. John Gai was a psychology professor at Humboldt State during our time there, and he did a lot of volunteer work in our neighborhood with homeless mentally ill folks. We had become acquainted with John through his wife, Gail, who worked at the Senior Resource Center. Gail and I shared interest in creative programs for retirees. At one point I was on a board of directors for a nonprofit mental health program that John had started. He was trying to coordinate a way for a person with mental health issues to be admitted to the lockup mental facility at the local hospital without having to go through a traumatic event that involved being taken to jail first.

It took a while, but John was able to link the mental health agency with the hospital and police department to issue a card to clients that allowed them to enter the hospital on their own. The card was good for 72 hours, usually enough time for the mental health emergency to subside. John told us that card saved Anthony and allowed him to live a more normal life. At the first sign of a manic episode, Anthony hauled himself to the lockup facility, where he presented his GET INTO LOCKUP FREE card and was immediately admitted. The poor man never had to pick a fight with a lumberjack again to get himself into a safe place. And it allowed Anthony to live a more normal life and keep thinking up creative projects for those in need.

21
Women in Management

At the beginning of my grant work, Mike taught me to use a camera. I documented all the projects as they took shape. One year I submitted a series of slides showcasing senior craftspeople to the California Arts Council, and that simple act pushed my work up a notch. The slide show became part of the Arts Council's promotional outreach to the State Legislature and opened a whole new world to me. From then on, I was invited to attended seminars and meetings around the state as aging programs began to proliferate.

One year I was invited to sit on a panel at a State House forum to prepare for a national hearing on aging issues in Washington, D.C. My panel mate was Dr. Erik Erikson, the famous psychologist and psychoanalyst, who was 95. I was familiar with Dr. Erikson's theories because I had subscribed to a psychology magazine for years and had a keen interest in brain science. I was stunned when Dr. Erikson's wife said to me during a break, "My dear, my husband and I are great fans of your work." Humboldt County is pretty remote so I wasn't aware that anyone outside the area knew about what I was doing. Whatever that was!

During a break in panel meetings I went to the State Capital. My brother-in-law worked in the state nursing home licensing department so I stopped in to say hello. Terry was surprised to see me and then lit up as he pointed to a stack of booklets. There on the cover was one of my photographs about the Wheelchair Container Garden project that I had just completed in a couple of nursing homes. I had known nothing about the article or how it found its way to Sacramento.

About a few years later I was even more stunned to learn from my sister, Eva, who worked as an administrative assistant to a powerful state senator who was chair of the Committee on Aging that I had been considered for a state job as liaison between two agencies. My sister didn't tell me about that until Mike and I were on our way to our new life in New Mexico. I asked why she had waited and she said, "I didn't want to spoil your plans. You seemed so excited to go live life as an artist." Turned out she was right.

About the same time as all that happened, I had another surprise: a newspaper reporter friend who had written numerous articles about my projects had, without my knowledge, submitted my name and programs to a National Associations of Counties award competition. I was dumbstruck when I received a call to show up at City Hall to meet the mayor. Even more so as I was presented with a plaque from the mayor with my name and that of a friend, who had also won the award for New Beginnings, a program focused on life skills for developmentally disabled folks. In the seventies, Humboldt County was a leader in the country for creative human services programs. Lillian Hoika and I shared the glory and have remained good friends.

Due to all the attention I received at the time, I was asked to sit on boards of directors for all sorts of nonprofit agencies in the area. I was also asked to join a group of prominent women in management. The women were bankers, lumber mill executive secretaries, newspaper reporters, and education executives. There was the executive director of the Humboldt Area Foundation and the director of the Humboldt Arts Council.

I was a bit eccentric in my choice of dress; most of my clothes came from the St. Vincent de Paul thrift store down the street from our flat. The women's group met monthly, usually in the boardroom of the host. We met for lunch and had topics for discussion. One month it was held at the Humboldt Area Foundation's stunning boardroom and the topic was "How to Dress for Success."

I can't remember being aware of the topic, or I would surely have made an effort to dress accordingly. To my horror, standing in the midst of a group of women in conservative suits, I looked down at my long denim skirt and fur-lined suede clogs and shouted, "Oh, my God, what am I doing here? Look, I really don't belong in this group." I was on the verge of tears as women began trying to comfort me. The Foundation secretary said gently, "We love you just the way you are, Charlotte. And we need to be reminded that it's okay to express one's self creatively by way of dress." There was a lot to be said about Humboldt County and the way everyone was free to express herself. We had never found another place as open and accepting of all people.

Eventually, it was my turn to host the monthly luncheon. Two Street, was a neighborhood in progress, so I was concerned that the Women in Management group might be apprehensive about dining at our place. Most of the women were old-timers who knew the reputation of the area, but to my delight, they all seemed eager to enter our world. There was a little shop around the corner from us that sold vintage clothing and other items from another era.

Charlotte Plantz

The store was owned by a young woman named Andi, whom I had met on my rounds of the neighborhood.

I told Andi about my upcoming lunch party, adding that I wasn't sure how to seat so many women in our many-roomed flat. She came up with the idea of setting up tables for four in several different rooms. And then she asked if I was interested in having a vintage clothing fashion show as entertainment. I jumped at the idea, and she said she had several friends who would love to model her clothes.

On the day of the luncheon Andi and her friends arrived early. I installed them in the rose-colored double bedroom with my old brass bed, which was covered in a painted velvet bedspread in various shades of dark red. It was quilted using heavy black satin thread. It was pretty garish on its own, but fit the bed and room perfectly. There was a red velvet boudoir chair with the "hooker" doll sitting in it.

Just as I poked my head in to see that the models had everything they needed, I heard one of them say, "Wow, doesn't this feel like our world." And then it hit me: OMG, the young women were high-class prostitutes. They weren't the hookers hanging out on the corners. No wonder they were free in the afternoon!

All I could think about was that the society editor of the local paper was about to ring my doorbell. There was nothing to do but go on with the show, and I never told anyone about my realization. My guests were thrilled with the table arrangements and the fashion show, and that luncheon became the hit of the year. I talked to Andi about it later and she revealed that indeed, she and her friends were "ladies of the night." And they were part of a program working with sexually abused girls. Andi said prostitution sometimes resulted from that type of abuse. We continued our friendship until we moved away.

During that same time, my friend Jane Hill and I were part of a tap dancing class that met several evenings a week and on Saturdays. I had become a dancing fanatic and attended class several times a week as we practiced and prepared for a big Fourth of July event. The tap teacher was short and round, but danced like Ginger Rogers. She and her six siblings had been regulars in musical films throughout their childhoods. That woman had us doing complex routines within the first week.

We were good! But I wound up getting cold feet (and stage fright) about tapping three miles over the Humboldt Bay bridges to the gazebo in front of our flat and dancing in front of a crowd. After all that work I refused to go on. The teacher and my classmates were furious with me, and I dropped out of the class. But it had a rather amusing end when I was invited to join the Soroptimists shortly after.

My friend Ellen from the Humboldt Area Foundation asked me to join Soroptimists International, a women's philanthropy group that was popular at the time. I told Ellen I didn't think that was my sort of thing, but agreed to go with her for a look. One had to be sponsored to become a member, and when it was Ellen's turn to introduce me, we both had to stand. I felt my face turning red as Ellen addressed the audience, "I want to introduce you to my friend Charlotte. She is an artist and director of a program for the elderly. She is also a tap dancer." Someone in the room piped up, "Oh, we have never had a tap dancer." Poor Ellen was terribly disappointed when I said, "Please don't make me do this." And she didn't, and I continued to be part of the Women in Management group and learned wonderful life skills that serve me to this day.

Charlotte Plantz

I met Tish Sommers in the spring of 1981 in Eureka. The two of us were part of a forum on displaced homemakers. The topic was of concern to the Area Agency on Aging because so many older women were being thrown into poverty when a spouse died or ran off with a younger woman. That is what happened to Tish at the age of 57. It was an epidemic during the sixties and seventies. When she told her story during the panel discussion, she became a folk heroine. The following year Tish became my mentor and I learned about her work with the Gray Panthers, an organization in Berkeley that focused on giving aid to displaced homemakers and marginalized older women. She also started OWL, the Older Women's League, which continues to this day.

Tish's unintended divorce left her with limited funds and no health insurance at a time when the youth culture had taken hold. In that era older women had become invisible and unemployable. Because Tish had been a homemaker her entire married life, she had no Social Security and had to rely on her ex-husband's financial generosity. The new divorcée had always been an activist for women's rights and did a lot of volunteer work so she had organizational skills. That day I met her, Tish told the audience a great story about her personal survival after her husband left. She said once the shock wore off she looked around at her immediate situation and realized she could not afford to keep her house.

Because Tish was part of numerous organizations that involved women of all ages, her story became a cause of sorts. A group of young women who shared a large rambling house in Oakland invited Tish to live with them. She said at first she couldn't imagine living with a group of twenty-somethings, but after thinking about it, and with no other options, she agreed to give it a try.

Me and My Magical Life

The audience and I roared with laughter when Tish said, "Ladies, I want to tell you that I got an education living with those young women. They convinced me that I should try everything! And I did. I opened up and became a better woman because of it. And I had a blast doing it." Tish Sommers was a hard act to follow but I did share a bit of my own story about how I had found my voice and some success as a displaced homemaker.

A funny event happened to me that day on my way to the panel discussion. I was driving down Two Street when a rather disheveled and inebriated young man ran out of a house in front of me. Fortunately, I was going slow and braked as he ran around to my open window. He stuck his head in the window and I smelled booze breath as he began reciting poetry in a strong Irish accent. It was a long poem and I knew I was going to be late, but didn't have the heart to stop the poet. When he finished reciting, the young man thanked me for listening to the poem he had just written. And he planted a kiss on my cheek and waved me off. I didn't know whether to laugh or cry but I knew I had to share the event at the panel discussion. Everyone laughed and applauded. Tish Sommers and I exchanged glances, and I knew we were destined to become friends.

The following year when I went to Sacramento for the state conference on aging, for some reason I hadn't made a hotel reservation. I had thought about staying with my sister, but then decided I wanted to be in the middle of the action. And then I forgot about it. I had always dreamed of staying at the Mansion Inn, a beautiful downtown garden hotel, but it was pricey so I hadn't even considered that option. I was at the registration table when someone asked where I was staying and I realized I had no place to stay. Embarrassed, I stammered, "Oh dear,

I don't know." And then I heard a voice addressing me by name. It was Tish Sommers, standing behind me. I turned and realized she had heard my announcement. Without hesitation, she said, "You're staying with me. I have a double room at the Mansion Inn and I would love your company." I was too stunned to argue.

We agreed to meet at the hotel that evening after a dinner meeting. When I arrived at her room Tish greeted me with a hug and pointed to a bottle of champagne and a big basket of fruit that an admirer had sent. We spent the evening talking and enjoying the bounty. It was then Tish told me that she had cancer. She said she wasn't afraid of death but did want to continue her activism. Tish Sommers died in 1985 at the age of 71.

Meeting her was a highlight in my life. Her work lives on, the best any of us could hope for. Between being on a panel with Dr. Erik Erikson and receiving his blessing and then staying with Tish Sommers at the Mansion Inn, my brain went into a heightened state. The conference was exhilarating and scheduled to go on for another day, but I was too stimulated, and I knew I had to hop on a plane and head home. It was the beginning of a series of over stimulations that pushed me toward a new life in a more tranquil setting.

That would not happen for a while. In the summer of 1981 we learned that Murray had committed suicide in Florida. His parents phoned us with the news and asked if they might come to Eureka to share their grief with us. Mike and I were stunned by his violent act and have never really gotten over the loss. Murray's parents told us their son was consumed by fear that he might wind up selling real estate to rich people in Florida. Murray had shared that thought with us several times over the years. Mike had met both parents during a hitchhiking trip to Florida with Murray in 1972. I talked on the phone with his father when I was in Mexico, but had never met the couple.

Murray's parents, Les and Molly, wanted to meet me in our home because their son had never stopped talking about the unusual friendship we shared. After getting a tour of our flat, Molly said, "Well, this explains everything. I see exactly why Murray was attracted to you. It was always about creativity." At the age of twenty-seven her son made the decision to keep from selling out. Our family continues to keep Murray in our thoughts, knowing he would love the way our lives turned out.

It occurred to me while writing about the Women in Management group that I had always had a "fashion line" attached to my life, and it had been based on the economy and what was at hand at the time. As a young woman I had sewed all my clothes and dressed like June Cleaver, the mom in the fifties sitcom Leave It to Beaver. There was no such thing as wash and wear fabrics; we sewed with stiff cotton fabric that had to be ironed. When I had two little daughters, between the three of us in our starched cotton dresses, my weekly ironing basket was piled high. As my sewing skills advanced I moved on to Vogue patterns and the latest fashion trends. Our circle of friends had been very social and we went out a lot, so that gave me an excuse to dress up. One time I even dyed a pair of high heels lavender to match an ensemble that I made to wear to an art house movie premier of the Pink Panther.

Not only had I sewed our clothes, fairly often I used fabric paint to decorate a sleeve or bodice. By fourth grade, Julie begged me to stop painting her clothes. Cyndi, on the other hand, said she loved her handcrafted outfits. By junior high school Julie complained that she dressed like a clown so I stopped. But I didn't stop knitting sweaters that made them stand out just as much. Poor children of an artist, they did suffer being different and having a parent who was too out of the mainstream, though on some level I knew they were proud of me.

The move to Half Moon Bay in 1966 didn't just establish me as a serious artist it also introduced me to a new friend, Berta Bray. I taught a batik fabric class that Berta attended and we hit it off immediately. My new friend taught home economics at the junior high school that Julie attended. Berta was a favorite among the students, boys and girls alike, because of her innovative and creative classes. Her cooking segment offered the latest culinary delights, and the sewing portion captured everyone's attention, turning out fashion accessories and wild stuffed dolls of every genre.

Berta introduced fabric painting and decorating techniques previously unknown to her students. Outside of her classroom, Berta and a friend started a hand-painted line of clothing known as Designing Women that has gone on for over fifty years.

Over the years, Berta and I did many trades. Once Berta dressed me in an extensive wardrobe of outfits that had not sold. She insisted that I accept the gift unconditionally. Were I to show up today in San Luis Obispo or any coastal city dressed in a Designing Women outfit, I would fit right in.

When I divorced in the early seventies, fashions leaned toward polyester and wrinkle-free fabrics. I was never able to adapt to that style and fortunately moved to New Mexico and a very different lifestyle. I had little or no money so wore what I had on hand and supplemented it from thrift stores. When I moved to Mexico I went back to sewing my clothes and painting or batiking fabrics in a myriad of ways. I taught a fabric printing class and used

Me and My Magical Life

a lot of different materials: cottons, velvet, linen, and rayon-or whatever was affordable. I became my own model in working out styles that complemented my fabrics. After Mike joined my class and began creating his own fabrics we bought a Singer sewing machine that was different from my old abandoned Kenmore. Mike taught me how to use and service the machine.

One day he surprised me with an African top he had sewn using one of his batik fabrics with a lot of machine embroidery. He told me that his mother had been a Singer sewing teacher and taught him to sew when he was young. Mike is color-blind, and my students were amused and impressed when I showed up in class wearing offbeat colored handmade clothing sewn by my husband. When we returned to Eureka two years later, I resumed buying my clothes in thrift stores. Once again we were low on funds, and I was burned out creatively.

Two years after moving back to New Mexico, once again I became a fashionista, and it had to do with my painted clothing. I created a line of painted tops and jackets that resulted in a married couple becoming my sales reps. Christine and Johnny Haddock were in the fashion business and were sales reps for a high-end line of imported ethnic clothing from around the world. They liked my work and asked to sell my line to some of their clients. Lucky me. Within a year or so Mike and I became close friends with Christine and Johnny. They lived in Dallas but had a house in Santa Fe where they spent holidays and summers. As usual, we had little money, so we were invited to spend a weekend now and then so Christine and Johnny could dress me in their last season's samples.

Each sample had a hole cut in it; that was how the couple avoided paying duty on the clothes they imported as samples. But holes didn't faze me because I had become an expert at patchwork. Christine and I met in a bedroom filled with racks of samples and she picked something she thought suited me. Then I strutted like a runway model through the living room where Johnny and Mike sat, and waited for their approval. Between the two of them, it was thumbs up or thumbs down. It was a simple process.

Sometimes we howled with laughter at some outlandish outfit that didn't suit me. Never had I witnessed two people derive so much pleasure from dressing a friend in free chic imported clothing. For years I was one of the best-dressed women in Santa Fe. And I was wearing all that Santo Domingo turquoise jewelry that I had obtained in trades for my handmade clothing..

Eventually I began painting and sewing my own clothing again. And Mike was printing my designs on T-shirts. He was also printing all the shirts for the United World College and had encouraged the art department to have students design their own shirts for different school events. The school highlighted countries by continent so they celebrated Asian Day, European Day, North American Day, South American Day, and African Day. The designs became more and more sophisticated and were popular and sought after. Mike and I always made sure we each had one of these shirts.

When I was in Wales for the wedding of a daughter of our friends the Maclehoses, her dad took me on a tour of Atlantic College, where he had taught. Atlantic College was the first of its kind and a model for others as they developed around the globe. The college is located in a stunning castle that overlooks Bristol Bay and was once owned by William Randolph Hearst. Andrew took me to meet the president, and in his castle tower office I noticed a large photograph on a wall. There were six students and one of them was wearing a T-shirt that Mike had printed. I let out a loud yelp and everyone laughed at the irony of my discovery.

At home I made sure my T-shirts were coordinated with a pair of pants or shorts, even when the T-shirt was ragged around the edges. I usually cut part of the bottom off and snipped a scoop neck, so over time, I started a new trend among students and friends. One day a potter friend stopped by, and as I greeted Douglas, he stood a moment staring at me. I asked what that was about and he said, "Wow, I just noticed that no matter how you dress it's always coordinated." I had to laugh because I was wearing an especially ragged T-shirt, but I did have to agree with him.

At my advanced age, I have a collection of painted and handmade garments I wear when the occasion calls for it, like a trip to coastal California. Or Santa Fe, a very hip place. Or Las Vegas, New Mexico, where you can show up in anything and feel comfortable. I also have a few treasured consignment/thrift store outfits that go back thirty or forty years and never seem to go out of style. To this day, you won't catch me without matching lipstick, a good haircut, and a shabby chic outfit. No wonder we have a little money in the bank. Not only do I pack my own tea bags (another creative pastime), I rarely pay retail for clothes.

22
Promotional Arts

A year after my first grant, Mike was ready to leave the security of Simpson Timber. Pulling green chain was taking a toll on his body. With both of us working, we had saved ten thousand dollars. When Mike quit work at the mill, I went to the bank and got a cashier's check for the full amount. The following day Mike put on a pair of overalls and I surprised him as I tucked the cashier's check into a top pocket. I turned him toward the stairs and challenged him to find a way to use the ten thousand dollars that would provide income. Mike was shy in those days, but I remembered a story he had told about his mom pushing him out the door every day when he was sixteen and being hesitant to look for a job. It hadn't taken long for him to get hired at a supermarket. And by the time my mate returned that evening, he had a plan.

Mike's brother-in-law worked for the local newspaper as an editor and knew everyone in the county, especially in the media world. Dale and Mike put their heads together and decided to approach Hobart Brown, the man who came up with the idea of a kinetic sculpture race on a grand scale. Innovative sculptures that were pedal-powered by a team of people were called kinetic sculptures. And they had to be seaworthy and hold up for three days and forty miles of rough terrain.

Charlotte Plantz

Mike and Dale asked Hobart if he would be interested in selling T-shirts promoting the race. The timing couldn't have been better; the business of T-shirt printing had just begun in big California cities. Hobart jumped at the offer, and the three men struck a deal. They would print twelve hundred shirts for the event. But first, Mike and Dale had to learn how to print T-shirts.

Our daughter, Julie's friend, Sean, was working in a new T-shirt printing facility in Sacramento. Mike hired Duane Flatmo, a young local artist, to design the shirt logo, and then he and Dale hightailed it to Sean's workplace to learn the fine art of printing T-shirts. Years before, Mike had worked for a company that silk-screened instructions on plastic, so he had a little experience. While we were in Mexico, a student's husband brought a simple silk-screen set-up for textiles that we wound up using for fabric designs in my class. In the seventies, silk-screen designs had to be hand-cut from acetate, and Mike turned out to be a master of that art.

The business took off, and we started in our apartment. Mike silk-screened in my studio and we hung the shirts to dry on a retractable clothesline that ran the length of our fifty-foot hall. And then we had to haul the shirts to a Laundromat where the ink was "cured" in hot dryers. Our landlord, Norton, offered Mike an old railroad car next to the dumpster in the alley as a shop for his business, but he outgrew that within a month. He moved into a large storefront space one street over and outgrew that within six months. Promotional Arts wound up in a huge Victorian building on the corner of Third and D, two blocks from our flat.

After searching for a business name, Mike and I came up with Promotional Arts because we wanted to represent local artists who were coming up with brilliant

Me and My Magical Life

T-shirt designs. And Mike had begun to do a few promotional radio and television ads for the business. One of his most successful radio ads was during the Valley Girl craze. He came up with the idea of having people bring in their "grodiest" T-shirts and he would print, for free, two Valley Girl quotes from among a variety of offerings, including "Grody to the max!" and "Gag me with a spoon!"

That ad came out one evening, and the next morning Mike nearly fell over as he turned the corner to the store. A line of people stretched halfway around the block, and everyone was holding a "grody" T-shirt. The store was well stocked with blank T-shirts, and Mike had hung samples of all the artists' shirt designs around the top of the walls. He did a brisk business that day with people buying blank shirts for more Valley Girl quotes. Mike soon became known for his clever promotional ads and for his skill in cutting stencils for six-color designs.

A lot of marijuana money was circulating in those days, and people kept coming up with creative ideas. One time Mike printed two-dozen six-color shirts with a rainbow and pot of gold as the theme. Each shirt had a person's name printed on the front. The buyer told Mike he was going to put the shirts in a box next to the co-op door in Garberville, where his friends were sure to find them. Another time Mike printed CAMP T-shirts for a bunch of growers. The acronym stands for Campaign Against Marijuana Production. At the time, helicopter raids were taking place all over the county. We had to laugh when a group of CAMP raiders came into the store and bought a bunch of shirts. And then held our breath that they wouldn't arrest Mike for printing them.

At the time, the Kinetic Sculpture Race was our biggest source of income. We were growing together as the race became known around the country. The smallest were two-man kinetic sculptures, and the numbers went up from there. One year, Hobart built an eight-person kinetic sculpture bus. Four men pedaled, while four scantily clad maidens managed the bota bags of Chianti. It was a three-day event that began in Arcata with a ten-mile ride to Eureka where they crossed Humboldt Bay. The sculptures had to be seaworthy, and some didn't make it. Once across the choppy bay, machines had to make it through the mudflats to the raging Van Duzen River. The pedaling teams had to navigate steep, muddy banks, usually in pouring rain, and then proceed to Ferndale and the finish line.

By the end of the race, more than one participant would suffer pneumonia. But that never stopped anyone from signing on the following year. The race had originally taken place Easter weekend, but the Coast Guard made Hobart move the race to a later date because of the danger involving flooded rivers. By then the Kinetic Sculpture Race had become an endurance test on a grand scale.

Hobart Brown was a character. He was eccentric, sexist, charming, witty, entertaining, and a barrel of fun. The artist had an art gallery on the first floor of an old Victorian house in downtown Ferndale and lived in a large apartment upstairs. Hobart was also a fine artist and a genius at getting people to work together artistically. The kinetic sculpture race was born out of an adult tricycle race held every year during the Fourth of July celebration in Ferndale. Hobart threw elaborate parties, usually with medieval themes. His upstairs apartment resembled a moody, dank castle, complete with a long dining table where he held baronial feasts.

Me and My Magical Life

Once a year Hobart organized a wild boar hunt in the area where such animals thrived. The catch was you had to hunt and kill using a spear. A lot of drinking was involved, though we never heard of anyone being injured. Somehow, every year there was a roasted wild boar in the middle of the baronial feast table. There were also serving wenches. Voluptuous women wearing low-cut medieval gowns flocked to Hobart's events. The women loved playing their roles as they flirted and filled tankards with mead. When Hobart Brown died, some of the air went out of Ferndale. He will never be forgotten.

Years later during a visit, Mike and I went to see the Kinetic Sculpture Race Museum in Ferndale. The first thing we saw was the original T-shirt that Mike had printed. It was hanging from the ceiling at the museum entrance. A young man approached us and stood searching our faces. His face lit up as he recognized Mike. He said, "Do you remember me? I'm Alex. I worked as an intern at Promotional Arts. You are the reason I became an artist." Our chosen name had lived up to its reputation; Alex wasn't the only person who became an artist because of Mike.

Mike had been printing silk-screened T-shirt art for a young Italian friend of Duane's whose father owned a vending machine business when something happened that would affect us all. One block down from our flat sat the old Vance Hotel. It was a huge, multistory ramshackle structure that had been built at the turn of the century. The building had been empty for years until the redevelopment project took place in Old Town. An eccentric wealthy man from San Francisco bought the hotel and to the horror of the city fathers, he painted it lavender. The owner shocked the city even further when he opened the hotel to homeless street people, allowing them to live there free of charge. Other than a few businesses on that block, we, along with the hotel dwellers, were the only people living in the neighborhood.

As with all redevelopment projects, it is understood that the transition takes a while. Fortunately, no people had lived in that part of Old Town for years so no one got displaced. The city plan was to gentrify the area by encouraging tourist-related shops, restaurants, and artists. Bars had always been part of the area, but they were urged to change their image and attitudes. Mike and I lived through the transition and couldn't wait to leave once the tourists and townies hit the streets. We felt our street people neighbors had better manners than some of those visiting the spiffed-up area. We felt lucky to have had the place to ourselves for seven years.

Once the tourists began to show up, the Vance Hotel stood out like a sore thumb. And that's when a turf war broke out. The Vance Hotel shared a boiler room with the Italian man's vending machine business on First Street. The room had a narrow enclosed bridge over the alley between the buildings. The hotel's only access to the boilers was through that bridge. The city pressured the Italian businessman to withhold use of the boiler, the source of heat and hot water for the hotel, so a very big deal.

The vending machine businessman sent some of his men to block the hotel access by boarding up the bridge. The hotel owner always had a crew working on the hotel, bringing it up to code, so in response he sent some of his workers with chain saws to cut a new door into the carriage house so they could access the boiler. The vending machine guy called it "a gorilla attack on his building." Lawsuits were filed and tempers flared as both sides dug in.

Me and My Magical Life

One rare sunny day, three men came to Promotional Arts and asked Mike to design a T-shirt for a group of hotel workers who now called themselves the Vance Guerrillas. They wanted an image of a gorilla wearing a bandolier and holding a chain saw. Mike loved the idea, because by then, the hotel saga was occupying the front page of the daily paper and people were choosing sides. Mike asked Duane to do the drawing of the gorilla for the shirt, but he refused because his friend, the son of the vending machine guy, asked him not to do it. The son actually came into Mike's store and told him not to print the T-shirts. When Mike asked why, the young man simply replied, "Have you ever heard of concrete galoshes?"

At that moment, who should show up but our old Montana friend, Barry McWilliams, who had become a cartoonist for weekly newspapers throughout rural America. We sent Barry to stay in our funky getaway trailer, where he could set up his cartoon workstation to stay on deadline. The morning after Barry's arrival, Mike and I walked down to the Two Street Café to have breakfast. When we opened the door we noticed the noise level coming from the back of the room. Seated at a large table, Barry had taken control of the Vance Guerrillas and they were talking about their takeover of the boiler room. Barry had already begun to sketch the gorilla design, and there were high fives as the image took shape. Mike and I were horrified by the excitement that filled the room. The turf war was about to begin. And we were caught in the middle.

Barry had a way of whipping people into action no matter what the event might be. In his eyes the more controversy the better. When Mike talked to him about the serious nature of the situation, he just laughed and continued to urge the Vance Guerrillas on. Mike and I were alarmed, because we had heard rumors of underworld connections. We were the only silk-screen business in the county and were being pressured by the Guerrillas on a daily basis. Finally, out of desperation I went to see our landlord.

In a rush of words I spelled out our dilemma to Norton, as he sat on the bottom step next to his shop door. He was quiet for a while and then looked up at me. I could see he was trying not to smile as he said, "Don't you worry. I'll take care of this." The next morning the doorbell rang and I was surprised to see Norton at our door. In his measured way, the old man said, "You tell Mike to print those Vance Guerrilla T-shirts." I thought about Norton's role in the neighborhood. We had never seen him in anything but his ragged clothes and dirty painter's cap, but apparently the man had the power of a titan. Old Town had been his domain from the time he was a boy, so he knew his way around the inhabitants.

For many years Humboldt County was known as a creative place, and marijuana played its part in perpetuating the image. With all that money floating around in the seventies, a lot of it was directed toward the arts, and that attracted a lot of talented people. When we arrived in 1976, the Humboldt Symphony was well established. There was a light opera company and three or four theater groups.

Humboldt State University was on the concert tour so top-rated performances became a standard. As our income grew we signed on for every season ticket series available. The art scene flourished and we were in the middle of it. Humboldt County soon had a reputation as one of the most artistically collaborative communities in the country. Artists loved working together..

Me and My Magical Life

Twenty-three years after we moved to New Mexico, Mike and I spent three months in Eureka. We were staying in the home of friends who had a place in Mexico. It was as though we had never left. We fell back into an artistic social life filled with old friends. Duane and Micki, his wife, insisted that we entertain and that's what we did. Mike and I had a memorable dinner party that was accompanied by a 6.5 earthquake that lifted us three feet on an undulating floor. Seconds later the huge jolt threw paintings off walls and glassware off shelves. Mike pushed me up against a doorframe and held me, saying, "Breathe, breathe." I barely squeaked, "It feels really big."

The quake hit one hour before our guests were due to arrive and power was knocked out so we had no way of knowing what was happening beyond our street. Oddly, within twenty minutes after the quake, Mike and I were completely relaxed. We ran outside and everyone was out on the lawns in shock. Mike had made a large pitcher of cosmopolitans, and once the shaking stopped we invited neighbors in for a drink.

It was one of the few dinner parties when I had everything prepared, but with an electric stove there was no way to warm the food. So the next-door neighbors scooped up the pans and took them home to their gas range. They waited until our guests arrived and returned with hot dishes.

We were stunned when our friends showed up and told their stories. John told of watching giant redwood trees being lifted three feet high with the rolling ground. John and Jan brought candles, lanterns, and wine. And Larry brought a framed photo of the Dalai Lama that he had shot in Bhutan a few years before.

Charlotte Plantz

Our guests sat in shock as I rattled on, telling funny stories. Saying goodbye, the Carroll's said, "We want you around for disasters because you are so calm and you have food and booze and tell funny stories." It turned out there was a lot of damage down along the bay.

Mike and Duane had become close during our early days in Eureka. They did a lot of work together at Promotional Arts, as Duane was much in demand as a T-shirt design artist. Forty years later, Duane and Micki are well-known artists who play a large role in Burning Man, the annual Nevada event. Duane and his friend Bill built a huge machine called El Pulpo (the octopus) that shot fire out of its eight arms. The arms were constructed out of old metal buckets stacked together. El Pulpo was so large, it required two semis to haul it to Burning Man. It took a crane to assemble the creature that burned up to two thousand gallons of propane during the seven-day gathering.

Duane and Bill have a new fire-breathing dragon and continue to be favorites with Burning Man fans. Over the years, Duane had made a name for himself as a muralist up and down the West Coast. And the Smithsonian Museum recently installed one of his kinetic sculptures. His wife, Micki, has an art gallery in Old Town Eureka and continues to dazzle viewers with her masterful paintings. My studio bathroom's primary color scheme comes from Duane's art hanging on the walls.

23
A Family Worth Remembering

Mike and I had driven by the Dwelley farm on Highway 101 many times before we finally stopped by. Over a year after our arrival in Eurkea, an ad in the local paper for U-Pick strawberries at the Dwelley farm finally motivated us to make the thirty-mile drive to Fortuna. Driving south on 101, we entered the steep Dwelley driveway right after crossing the Van Duzen River bridge; a rather hair-raising experience. To make this turn we had to cut our speed from 65 mph to about 25 mph within two hundred feet, and often there was a log truck on our tail. Fortunately, there was a right turn lane to their driveway, but it was short and if we went too fast we had to make another hair-raising U-turn and drive north for a mile or so to turn around on an overpass and make another attempt.

The Dwelleys' driveway was a metaphor for life in the mid-seventies on their farm in Humboldt County. From the time we met the family, everything about their life was rather hair-raising on a regular basis. It was a chilly, foggy summer day the first time we drove to the farm. Mike and I met Chuck and his five-year old daughter, Kendra, or K.C. as she was called at the time. K.C. was wearing rubber boots and she kept up a running dialogue about life on the farm as we moved slowly through the mud and damp strawberry plants, filling our pails to overflowing. K.C. schooled us on the art of growing berries and raising sheep. The little girl made sure to let us know how hard they worked.

As we grew to know the family, their hard work became apparent. We didn't meet Chuck's wife, Sally, or his toddler son, Matt, until another time. Until then, we had to deal with way too many strawberries. All that chatting had diverted our attention from the task at hand. But we were smitten with the five-year-old and warmed to her dad.

I was involved with the Senior Resource Center at the time and there was a lunch program for seniors that sourced local produce for the kitchen. It didn't take me a moment to recommend the Dwelley farm for berries and vegetables. Chuck and Sally were grateful for the opportunity, and over time we became close friends. The couple and their children loved coming to town to have dinner with us, and we enjoyed driving to their farm for the same reason. If it was dinner at our place, Chuck brought a huge bag of produce from their gardens and usually a bag of potatoes or rice. He said that was because he needed a lot of fuel to support his high-energy level and didn't expect other people to fill him up. Money was tight for the four of us in those days, so when we went to their place we took cheap jug wine.

When the third Dwelley child was born, they named her Lindsay, and once again Mike and I were smitten. Lindsay was eight months old when we had the family to dinner to celebrate my birthday. I bought little gifts for everyone and we decorated the table with party hats and noisemakers. I had tinted a three-tier birthday cake bright purple and baked it in Mexican cake pans. The icing was white with red decorations and forty birthday candles. To this day, we laugh about Lindsay's first solid food being purple cake, even knowing what we now know about food coloring. Lindsay just earned a PhD in psychology, so as far as we know she was not adversely affected. The wonderful thing about sharing a meal with the Dwelley family was, and is, the sheer delight in being together. During that time when the children were small, it was usually loud and boisterous and we most always laughed ourselves silly.

As is common among our friends and family, there is a tradition that continues: we always have happy hour at five o'clock prior to dinner, with drinks and appetizers and a lot of conversation. In those early days, appetizers at the Dwelley farm might consist of soda crackers with blue cheese. I remember one evening when Chuck brought out the cheese, saying they could only afford enough for us adults. The children were upstairs playing in their rooms, when all of a sudden they smelled the cheese and came running and shouting, "Blue cheese, hooray, blue cheese." We were laughing so hard at little Matt and K.C. drooling over blue cheese we handed it over to them. I don't think there was a food they wouldn't eat. They were fortunate to live on a farm and grow much of their food.

Chuck had degrees in horticulture and international business so he knew what he was doing. It was just much harder to farm in Humboldt County, where it rained most of the time or was shrouded in fog. And then there were the gophers. Chuck and Sally had planted one thousand artichoke plants, a costly investment, but one suited to the climate. Just as the plants showed some promise, the couple watched from their window as every single one of them was pulled under ground by gophers. For a while it seemed that every crop they tried was undone by some unforeseen calamity.

Charlotte Plantz

One year on December 23, our daughters were visiting for Christmas when a cyclone blew in over the county. The four of us had been out for an early evening walk in unusually warm weather along the bay. There was not a hint of breeze, and we agreed it felt eerie enough to head home. We barely made it as a strange wind picked up and made our hair stand on end. We were nervous by the time we reached the top of the stairs and hurried to the living room. The four of us stood in front of the big windows peering out at the street below.

A couple had just walked past a huge plate glass window in the building across the street, and we watched in horror as the window blew out in slow motion. We could see individual pieces of glass in an arc as though shot from inside the empty building, barely missing the now running couple. We each ran to a bedroom away from the windows, but we were terrified of the skylight that loomed twenty feet above the long hall. The howling wind shook the entire building for a long time, but the skylight held. Finally, we came back together, and amid nervous laughter, counted our blessings.

The Dwelleys' farm had not fared as well. Once the hurricane-force winds died down we gathered in the kitchen to start dinner. All we could talk about was what had just occurred, and then we remembered the Dwelleys. I ran to the phone and held my breath as it rang. And it rang for a while, boding bad news. Finally, Chuck picked up and I nearly shouted, "Are you guys all right?" There was a long pause and then in a shaken voice Chuck gave me the details: "The wind picked up the barn roof and turned it clockwise and then set it back down, about a quarter off center. It's bad." The Dwelleys' barn is one of the largest in the county so that was a big deal. Chuck went on to say the wind had also dismantled the

230

neighbor's shed and thrown boards on top of a newly planted field. The family had no electricity so the water pump was out. And the entire family had the flu.

So that was our dinner conversation as we pondered how to help our friends down the road. Julie was in nursing school so she was eager to help the flu patients. Mike and Cyndi made a plan to clean up debris and I took a chicken out of the freezer for a big pot of healing soup. Christmas Eve found our little family spread out around the Dwelley farm, doing what we could to lighten their load. We were so involved with our friends that Mike forgot to check his store on Third Street. He had just moved in and was ready to resume business, so we were relieved to find it intact when we stopped by on our way back from Fortuna.

Finally, Chuck had begun to make progress with his production vegetable crops. He had a contract with Safeway for zucchinis and invested in a large number of seeds. We watched as the plants grew and seemed to thrive in the iffy weather. When Chuck took his first harvest to Safeway he was devastated to learn they would only take perfectly straight, six-inch zucchinis. There weren't that many straight ones so he had to sell out of his pickup truck along the streets of Fortuna. Amazingly, Chuck worked out a deal with a logging company that allowed him to ship boxes of zucchinis on a lumber truck headed to the Bay Area.

Our poor friend tried every vegetable he could think of and finally gave up. The couple wound up leasing land to a dairy farmer. And then Chuck and Sally went back to school for teaching credentials. They spent the next twenty years teaching in local elementary schools. But not before a near-death experience for Chuck.

Charlotte Plantz

Chuck was a runner. He ran every day and decided to train for a marathon. Chuck usually ran with Jill Irvine, wife of their family doctor. Jack and Jill lived on a farm a few miles south of the Dwelley farm. Jack was not a runner so he stayed with the children. Early one foggy winter morning Jill was running alone on a narrow back road. The mother of four-year-old twin girls was hit and killed by a drunk driver, a horrible tragedy that shook the community, especially Chuck and Sally, who had become close to the Irvines. Three weeks after Jill's death, Dr. Jack had to tell his dear friends that Chuck had stage-four melanoma cancer. The doctor thought Chuck had maybe six weeks to live. Chuck phoned us the next day and as we sobbed together we tried to make sense out of the latest tragedy.

After the loss of their friend, Jill, Chuck was in a low place, made more so because they had no health insurance, no life insurance, and little money. And they had no wood for their only source of heat in winter. We continued to cry and came up with no reason why the family kept having so many traumas. A few days later Mike and I sat with Sally in the Fortuna hospital waiting room while Jack performed a biopsy on Chuck's liver. If the cancer had spread to that organ Chuck would surely die soon. We wouldn't learn the outcome until the following day. It was an excruciating wait. Thankfully, when the call came it was good news versus a negative outcome; there was no sign of cancer.

Jack decided to send Chuck to Moffitt Hospital in San Francisco for a series of procedures to stimulate his immune system. Immunology therapy was a new idea that had won favor with cancer specialists. Chuck was excited to be included in the first trials. Our friend spent the next year driving 275 miles to San Francisco every three months for injections of a selected disease to his back. The dose was just enough to set the disease in motion and allow his immune system to fight it off. The poor guy had huge pustules erupting all over his back for days as his body fought the onslaught.

Almost immediately, the Fortuna community came together and took care of many needs for the Dwelley family. People brought truckloads of firewood. A steady stream of hot dishes and desserts were delivered, but most of all an abundance of love and compassion was wrapped around the family during the worst of all hair-raisers. And it worked! Chuck made a complete recovery. The immunology therapy was a success and forty years later has become standard treatment for some forms of melanoma.

One of the highlights of our time in Old Town was having the Dwelley children spend one weekend a month with us to give their parents a break. At that time, Lindsay was four years old, K.C. was eleven, and Matt was six. They were considered old enough to ride the bus the thirty miles from Fortuna to Eureka. One of their parents put them on the bus and then phoned us with their arrival time. Mike and I waited at the stop as the children filed off with their little suitcases in hand. It was an exciting adventure for us all.

Our huge flat had plenty of room for guests, and Old Town offered a city experience for rural farm children. We had a lot of window display paraphernalia from a local department store that provided hours of creative play for the children, and I had an old felt dress dummy covered with various pins and brooches that was a favorite. The five of us were sure to have lunch at Two Street Café, and the children's going-out clothing was decorated with pins and brooches.

Charlotte Plantz

As an adult, K.C. recalled memories of that time as joyful events. A recent note from her is worth sharing: "One favorite memory I had was roller skating with you guys on First street in Old Town. I also remember going to a boxcar on the railway to buy trinkets and scouting Saint Vincent de Paul's thrift store for great treasures. Being with you transformed the ordinary. I remember being in your studio with the big windows overlooking the plaza and the woman model's torso with all the pins."

"You gave Lindsay a pin with what looked like oil in it that was black and when you pressed it, rainbows appeared. One time, you were wearing rainbow socks when a rainbow appeared over the bay and I thought it was magical at the time, just like in the Xanadu movie. So much of what you and Mike did was magic." We still laugh remembering little Lindsay ordering a bowl of Texas chile and staying with it in spite of the heat. Her parents were a bit horrified hearing that report, but allowed them to visit the following month.

The Dwelley farm had a lot of fruit trees, including a variety of apple trees. Every fall for a few years Mike and I gathered with the family to make apple pies for our freezers. The four of us went in on an apple peeler/corer device that clamped onto a table edge. It was a good way to deal with a lot of apples at one time. It also made a big, sticky mess, with apple peels spilling out of the pan and juice running down onto the operator's legs and onto the floor. I was in charge of turning out pie dough at an alarming rate while Mike turned the peeler. Chuck and Sally filled the pie shells and sealed the tops. We started early in the morning and didn't stop until we had around twenty pies. It was exhausting but highly satisfying. And we always baked a pie to go with our supper at the end of the day. We had Chuck to thank for mopping up the sticky mess.

Me and My Magical Life

New Year's Day turned into a short-lived tamale-making tradition at the Dwelley farm. It was also the day Chuck had programmed the ewes to lamb. To add to the excitement, the Van Duzen River was usually at flood stage. The first time Mike and I witnessed that event we were looking out the kitchen window toward the river, several hundred yards north of the house. An optical illusion made the river appear to be higher than the house, a disturbing sight until Chuck explained the phenomenon. On that particular New Year's Day Mike and I had spent the night so we could get an early start on tamale making and lambing.

Chuck and Mike headed out in a freezing drizzle and found lambs dropping on the ground all over the field. Sometimes newborn lambs need help breathing, and the solution is to swing them around by their legs until they get their first breath. At one point in the early morning, Mike, covered with blood and placenta, stuck his head in the kitchen door and shouted, "There are lambs coming out in pairs. I just had one in each hand, swinging them round and round until they caught their breath. Gotta go, Chuck just yelled for help with triplets. I'm having a blast."

By the time the tamales were steamed and ready to serve, it dawned on Sally and me that we hadn't planned anything to go with them except beans. We hadn't made chile gravy to go on the tamales, so we sat around the table munching a rather dry meal. No one seemed to mind except Sally, who kept saying, "We really should have fixed a salad." The kitchen was warm and damp and smelled earthy despite the men having washed up. Dinner conversation was lively, and the children wanted to hear all the gory details of delivering lambs on New Year's Day.

Charlotte Plantz

One especially warm, sunny summer weekend we joined the Dwelley family for a camping trip to the Mattole Campground near the Lost Coast. Signs directed campers to various locations, including one that read "clothing optional." K.C. shouted, "Let's go skinny-dipping. Please, let's do it." Mike and I had been going to College Cove, a skinny-dipping beach in Trinidad that was a favorite of Humboldt State University students. During those years, there was so little sun in summer, the moment any of us saw a break in the fog we high-tailed it to that beautiful cove and threw off our clothes. K.C. had heard us talk about that with her folks and thought it a great idea. Chuck agreed, but Sally was apprehensive. She considered it for a bit, and then decided she wanted to have the experience.

Mike would be happy if he never had to wear clothes so he was our point man; the minute we got settled in to our campsite, Mike was in the river. I hesitated because of Sally but decided to go for it, and that was all K.C. needed. She whipped off her clothes and jumped in with me. The little girl was around seven years old, and I held her flat and floated her. There were ferns along the banks and it was sun-dappled and shady-and gorgeous. K.C. was completely relaxed and called to Sally, "Mom, if the ranger comes we can tell him we are fish disguised as people." That's all it took. Sally and Chuck threw off their clothes and jumped in, taking turns to float little Matt in their arms. Sally declared it a milestone.

Recently, Chuck and Sally told us about a Thanksgiving dinner conversation last year when their adult children asked about those weekend getaways. The big question was how their parents came to trust us enough to hand their children over for a weekend. And the answer is why I wanted to write about the

Me and My Magical Life

Dwelley family and what a special friendship it has been for us all because it almost always included the children. And then I realized that it had been the same with all our old friends; the children had always been a big part of the relationship. And remain so to this day.

24
The Getaway Retreat

Because our life was pretty much restricted to Old Town, I began to feel claustrophobic and in need of fresh air. Our flat was directly in front of a paper mill across the bay, where a steady stream of toxic pulp fumes blew most of the time. The primary ingredient in paper manufacturing is chlorine, and in those days it was an unregulated process. The smell was horrible, like dirty socks, especially when the wind blew our way. It turned out that chlorine made a lot of people sick, and by the time we moved away I had become one of the victims. Until that happened, I developed a lot of allergies that plague me to this day. Fortunately, after enough public outrage the paper mill was closed shortly after we moved.

Instinct told me that we needed to find a way to get away from the city and its toxic fumes on weekends, so I put out the word. It didn't take long before a woman approached me to tell me about the perfect place. Barbara knew a lot of people in the county and was a bit of a hustler, something that grew more pronounced as time went on.

Barbara told me about her ranch friend's old trailer in the Arcata Bottoms; wetlands and estuaries where the bay emptied and filled with the tide. Christensen's ranch bordered Lanphere Dunes, part of the Humboldt Bay

Charlotte Plantz

National Wildlife Refuge, a spectacular narrow strip of land between the Bottoms and Pacific Ocean. The ranch was only ten miles from Eureka, but a wilderness world away by any stretch.

Barbara accompanied us to meet Chris and take a look at his rental. It was the funkiest old trailer with vines growing up inside the walls. Mike and I were shocked by the degradation, but as we stood on the crude front porch and took in the views, we knew we were going to take it. From the back, a series of sloughs ran off in different directions, and at low tide white egrets lined up to herd schools of fish to the ends of the sloughs, where they were easily picked off. To the left of the trailer, grazing pastures were filled with beef cows and standing egrets.

Once, when a cow died, we awoke to see a dozen huge vultures perched among the snowy white egrets in the tall eucalyptus trees lining the pasture. At the edge of one of the sloughs an oyster farm had taken hold. Across the road the Lanphere Dunes seduced us with trails into a miniature dune forest, where lichen glowed in the dark on a full moon night. Mike and I were smitten. Even more so when we learned the rent would be one hundred fifty dollars a month.

One of the first things we found for our new digs was a freestanding fireplace at St. Vincent de Paul for twenty-five dollars. Between the nearby ocean and the water-filled estuaries, Christensen's ranch felt like a cold steam bath that saturated every corner of the old trailer. In dense fog you could actually see water droplets. That was the air we were breathing. As Mike and I put on a few pounds we figured it was from all the water we were ingesting. We were literally plumped up!

A friend who had a creative recycling center in Santa Rosa was forever giving us surplus goods she collected from various industries around the Bay Area. One of those was a satin sheet manufacturer. Susan asked if we could use a pile of satin remnants, and because I could never turn down a potential creative project I gladly accepted her offer. When Mike and I picked up the fabrics, Susan said she also had remnants of quilt batting from the same company. My brain fairly flew to a creative solution for the freezing trailer bedroom. One nice thing about a twelve-room flat was that we had plenty of room for Susan's offerings.

Mike and I checked with Chris about installing a fireplace and upholstering the bedroom walls of his funky rental. The man admitted that it was so bad anything would be an improvement. We spent a weekend stapling strips of thick quilt batting on the walls and then I sewed endless strips of water-stained rose-colored satin that we stapled over the batting. Actually, it turned out to be quite exotic, in a Playboy Mansion way, but best of all, it covered all the cracks and warmed the room.

Mike built the bed above a storage unit with drawers so we could lie in bed and look out the window and watch the tide roll in and out of the slough. That inspired us to buy glow-in-the-dark stars to put on the ceiling. There was a guide for aligning the stars into constellations, and Mike was proficient at that task. During a visit when the Dwelley family came to our funky trailer, four-year-old Matt was taken into the bedroom to look at the starry ceiling. The child studied the constellations for a while and then announced, "Look, there is Draco."

As soon as Mike closed the store on Fridays we hit the road for Arcata and our hideaway. We kept a supply of canned groceries on hand and hauled fresh produce and fish from town. Late one Saturday afternoon we had

Charlotte Plantz

a call from Barbara announcing she and a friend were escorting four California Arts Council members to our getaway place. They were in town for a regional meeting. The Sacramento group was staying at our flat because they wanted to spend some time with us, and they were disappointed we wouldn't be staying in town with them. Mike and I could not bear to give up our weekend at the ranch, so we invited them to dinner at our retreat. And they had a map.

We had not invited Barbara, who was at their meeting. When she asked the Arts Council group where they planned to have dinner and learned it was with us, she offered to lead them to our place. Barbara's invitation created a problem, especially because she was not alone. Not only was our funky trailer small, I had just enough food for six. Mike had run to town and was supposed to bring a big salmon from home, but he forgot. I had half an hour to come up with a dinner plan for eight.

My friend Berta's dad had told me a long time ago that if I wanted to impress dinner guests I should serve fried potatoes with onions. Berta's mom and dad used to host huge gatherings of up to two hundred fifty San Francisco movers and shakers at their ranch for hunts of various kinds. Her dad told me their guests loved those potatoes and onions, and it was something I never forgot.

Suddenly I had a plan; I had a stash of canned salmon and a bag of potatoes. I also had a six-pack of shortcakes, two pints of berries, and a half pint of whipping cream. I ran next door to our biologist neighbor and asked if he had anything to augment my dessert plan of English trifle. Bless Dave he had a package of instant custard. The dessert was complete. I was relieved to find onions, so Mike peeled potatoes and sliced onions while I put together salmon patties. We had a fire in the fireplace and soft music playing as the group arrived.

Me and My Magical Life

A thick fog had rolled in and it was cold. The combined potato and onion smells along with frying salmon patties permeated the air. When the first person entered the room they nearly swooned. Berta's dad was right. Those folks were hooked. One of our guests was a Cheyenne Indian from Wyoming and he said he nearly wept as he walked in the door. The aromas took him back to his childhood and wrapped around him like an old Indian blanket. The group had brought wine, and packed like sardines, we declared the dinner party a howling success. But I began to pay more attention to Barbara and how she kept slipping into my life at awkward moments.

A walk through the dune forest was sure to conjure up images of hobbits and elves hiding among the stunted pine trees and the mushroom- and moss-covered ground. And suddenly, there would be a dramatic change as pine trees were engulfed in sand dunes that rose in front of us to great heights. It was not easy to clamber up their steep sides, but the sound of pounding surf promised even more drama on the other side.

During winter after a huge storm, redwood trees washed up on the beach like pick-up sticks, along with piles and piles of driftwood of every size and shape. And once, the carcass of a deer, but never did we meet another human being.

Now and then a gift bag of oysters appeared on our porch, and we foraged for other delicacies in the area: clams, salmon, chanterelle mushrooms, blackberries, and huckleberries. Wild rhododendrons and azaleas lined the back roads, permeating the air with their heady fragrance. A day hike could yield a complete meal with flowers for the table. Humboldt County is, to this day, an experience to delight all the senses. For us, it was a treasure trove that continued to fill us with gratitude for the experience.

Charlotte Plantz

Except for my old nemesis Barbara, who over time became aggressive in trying to use my reputation for her own gain. In one bizarre incident, she showed up with a pair of gloves she had bought at St. Vincent de Paul. She claimed she found a woman's beautiful wristwatch inside one of the gloves and insisted on giving it to me. I had recently remarked that I needed to buy a new watch, but I refused her offer as I reflected on her growing brazenness.

Relentless, Barbara next tried to badger me into supporting some shady idea of hers. When I refused, she became hostile and began to argue with me. By then, I had had enough. Anger propelled me to usher the intruder out the front door. That pesky woman was one of the reasons I began to think about leaving our ideal life in Old Town.

Barbara wasn't the only one provoking the idea; our landlord, Norton, had become testy with me. I was on a local TV program on aging now and then and in the local newspaper too often for Norton's liking. Mike and I had become too successful. He had a soft spot for humble folks and to him, we had moved beyond that. When the local television station asked to do a feature story about our time on Two Street and the renovation of our home, that was the final straw for Norton.

After seven and a half years, Norton Steenfott asked us to move. That was a huge shock to us, and we felt betrayed because of all the work we had done on his flat. At that moment, Mike and I knew that we had to own our own place, but California housing prices were out of our reach. Becoming well known had become a liability for me. And that is when the image of New Mexico began to loom large in my imagination. But there was one more event that put the thought into motion.

25
The Senior Resource Center Extravaganza

In 1980 the Eureka School District handed over to the Senior Resource Center a three-story school that had been closed for years. The school was near downtown and accessible by city bus. It took over a year to renovate the facility so it could be used as a senior center. Fortunately, there had been a cafeteria in the basement so that was easily turned into the center dining facility. A section of the basement became the first Alzheimer's Day Care Center in the country. One of my jobs was to provide rotating senior art shows on the walls of the entry hall into the facility.

The Alzheimer's Day Care Center director had trained in Sweden and she introduced a whole new concept: the room was filled with comfortable couches and chairs. The walls were covered with art. A long formal dining table and chairs provided space for craft projects and snacks. It was a lovely environment for all involved; families could drop off loved ones for several hours, providing respite for caregivers and meaningful activities and socializing for clients.

The entire community was excited about the new senior center, so the staff decided to throw a huge opening party once everyone had moved in. I was chosen to organize the party: All of it. It was a dream come true for my energy at the time so I jumped right into the task. One of the first issues was music. It was June, and as I called around I found that every music group in the county had a commitment for graduations and weddings. Finally I called our young musician friend Duane Flatmo, who told me he and his band would be happy to play for the event.

However, my excitement was dashed when Anne and Bev said we couldn't possibly have the Male Chauvinist Marching Pig Band entertaining a bunch of old people. When I called Duane back he laughed and said the band would play familiar old tunes for the crowd. When I reminded Anne and Bev that Duane's band was the only game in town, they had to agree.

With music out of the way I moved on to refreshments, making endless calls to get the best deals. It was up to me to get the program printed, and once again, being June, with graduations and weddings, every printer in Eureka and Arcata was booked. Out of desperation I stopped by a newspaper office and begged for help. As I introduced myself, the printer stepped out of the back room and stood listening to my plea. He smiled as he said, "You are the only person in the county that I will stop the press for to help you out." The woman at the counter and I nearly fell over. The printer added that he was an admirer of my work with elderly folks and eager to help. I was on a roll.

My big plan was to decorate the three-story building using art and crafts from all the creative seniors I had come to know. A group of women had formed a miniature quilt club. My idea was to hang their quilts on the stair walls to showcase their work and brighten up the place. I had worked with an incredible photographer as a

Me and My Magical Life

home health aide and grouped her black-and-white photos on one large wall. Painters in every medium picked their best pieces for a grand art show throughout the building. Nurseries donated large potted trees and shrubs, so by the time of the opening the old school house had been transformed. It was, quite simply, beautiful. I saw dignitaries wipe tears from their eyes as they roamed the rooms and I was filled with joy.

Duane's Male Chauvinist Marching Pig Band was a huge hit. They had folks on their feet dancing to their favorite tunes, and the crowd fell in love with them. There were a lot of speeches and acknowledgments, and when my turn came I fled to the empty basement. I could not bear to have my name announced in front of all those people, so Anne had to make an excuse for me.

I knew then that my mania had run out, and I was about to begin a downward spiral. Again, I thought of moving away from an ideal life. Sadly, I became quite ill for a while so I decided to make a trip to Northern New Mexico alone to sort out my thoughts. As so often happens in my life, at just that moment I had a letter from Bessie Abeyta, my dear friend and former landlady in Chacon that summer of 1972.

Bessie and I had communicated throughout the years, and she always reminded me that my little adobe house was still there and available whenever I might want it. After talking with Mike, I decided to drive to New Mexico and spend the month of October on the side of the mountain in my little old adobe house. Over the phone, Bessie and I fantasized about wandering the fields during Indian summer and picking bouquets of wildflowers while we chatted about life.

That did turn out to be a fantasy because the second day I was there it began to snow. It turned so cold the produce I had bought froze in the little refrigerator. I had always been a quick-change artist, so without hesitation I decided to visit old friends in Santa Fe for a few days. I phoned Zenia and Gaylon, and they were happy to have me as their guest. The couple introduced me to some wonderful iconic events in the City Different, and I felt again the pull the place had on me.

On my way back from Santa Fe I stopped in Las Vegas to visit Joe and Diana Stein in their bookstore on the Plaza. We had been friends ten years earlier when they had a store called Chicken River that sold all sorts of counterculture goods. It was a fun store but didn't go over so well with the locals, so Joe and Diana set out to create a different image.

Beneath their counterculture veneer the couple turned out to be scholars. Over the years they had collected out-of-print Western books on every subject and actually had enough books to open a store. They bought a storefront in Old Town that had a lovely little apartment in the back and made a name for themselves as rare Western booksellers. A woodstove sat in the middle of the store, and Diane served tea to customers who wandered in from the street.

My old friends were delighted to see me, and Diana put the kettle on as I settled into a chair in front of the stove. We had a lot to catch up on, and their big news was about the United World College of the American West that was about to open. The Occidental Petroleum oil magnate, Armand Hammer had recently paid for the old Montezuma Castle property near Las Vegas to be turned into a two-year prep school for students from around the world. Hammer also put up money for scholarships.

Two hundred students from fourteen countries would be chosen through academic testing so that the brightest applicants, regardless of social standing or income, would have the opportunity for higher education. Prince Charles was the board president of the United World College system that had begun fifteen years earlier in Wales, UK. Andrew Maclehose had been chosen as dean and would get the school up and running.

I could hardly believe what I was hearing as Diana and Joe continued to fill me in on details. They had been told that Prince Charles would attend the opening, and Armand Hammer had arranged to have the Beach Boys perform. I later learned that Andrew Maclehose was not too happy about the spectacle that was unfolding around him. It was the exact opposite of his philosophy for the school and for him personally.

But it did endear the dean and the school to the community. Having a prince and the Beach Boys in Las Vegas on the same day would go a long way toward Las Vegans embracing a bunch of foreigners in their midst. For my part, the very thought of a slew of foreign young people dropping in on the little city of Las Vegas had my heart racing. It also sweetened the prospect of a move for Mike and me.

A strange feeling came over me as I sat with Joe and Diana in the warmth of the stove, sipping tea. I had a powerful sensation that had to do with the Maclehose family; I knew we were destined to meet and become friends. When we did meet and become friends, I told Andrew about the thought I had that day in the bookstore. He laughed and said he did not believe in that sort of nonsense. However, over the years, as he and his wife, Heather, grew to know us, they would become less surprised by that kind of nonsense.

When I had driven out of Chacon on my way to Santa Fe it had been daylight, and there were no cows around the place. I arrived back in the dark and didn't stop at the Abeytas' house. It was freezing and essential that I get a fire started; the adobe walls had absorbed the cold and it would take a couple of days to warm them up. Mike had insisted I take a pair of down pants and top as well as down booties. Once I changed into those and stopped shivering I was able to function.

During that time I was doing a lot of writing and enjoyed the solitude so I didn't feel lonely. Once I got the fire banked in the woodstove, I crawled into bed wearing the down suit and promptly fell asleep. Sometime around four a.m. I had to pee. The urge woke me up yet I couldn't bear to get out of bed to drop those down pants, even for a moment. But just as I could barely hold it any longer, I heard footsteps outside the window. My heart began to race, along with my thoughts.

I flew out of bed, turned on the lights, and ran to the chamber pot. At first I thought it must be my imagination, but then I heard the footsteps again-right outside the window. There was another window at the end of the kitchen area to the west. I opened the shade to total darkness and then saw a light come on at the Abeyta house a quarter of a mile below me. I knew immediately that Pedro was aware of my predicament and it calmed me down. I also knew that if he believed someone was walking around my place he would be right up. Pedro and I had always had an interesting relationship that involved a lot of magic and I trusted that. The next hour until the crack of dawn I spent writing poetry as the footsteps continued on the other side of the wall. By then, I had decided if it was a person, they would have broken in by that time.

With the first ray of light, I opened the shade of the window where I'd heard the footsteps and peered out. To

Me and My Magical Life

my relief, I saw Pedro's cattle milling around in the morning mist. I laughed, realizing Pedro must have put the cows in while I was away. He was forever moving cattle from one grazing area to another. When I went down to have breakfast with Bessie and Pedro I told the story of footsteps in the night and we had a good laugh. Pedro said he woke up when my light went on and knew exactly what had transpired. And that was what I adored about the little old man. Pedro said, "I knew you would figure it out and not be afraid. That's why I didn't come up."

During my stay in Chacon I was living in a house a mile or two away from the house where I had spent the week with my nun friend ten years earlier, throwing questions out to the wind. So I decided to do the same thing for the next few days; I questioned wanting to give up a wonderful career and ideal life in order to live an artistic life in a challenging place as I was about to turn fifty. I questioned the financial implications and the reality of starting completely over again in a foreign land. As before, the wind blew the answers back to me, and I drove back to California determined to make it happen.

26
Santo Domingo Connection

In June of 1982, with our enthusiasm intact, Mike and I set out on a road trip from Eureka to Northern New Mexico. We were seriously scouting the area with a move in mind for the following year. Mike's silk-screen business was thriving, and my hand-painted and silk-screened clothing line was taking off but we were feeling the need for change. The idea for the trip was to determine whether we could start over again in the Land of Enchantment. Our first stop was in Santa Fe, where we strolled around looking for inspiration. I was wearing one of my floral silk-screened, quilted vests that usually got people's attention. Little did we know how that would affect our life as we approached the portal of the Palace of the Governors on the Plaza.

Every square inch of the portal was taken up by Native American jewelers and potters from the surrounding Pueblos. Artists were lined up along the back wall, sitting on stacks of blankets or folding chairs, with their artwork spread out in front of them. Mike said he was going to wander around side streets and check to see whether there were any silk-screen shops. I chose to stay at the portal and check out the goods being offered.

I was squatting down in front of a blanket covered with beautiful turquoise jewelry when I heard a voice directed at me. A woman said, "Hey, where did you get that vest?" I was completely surprised by the question and it took me a moment to formulate a response. When I told the woman I had made it, she continued, "Hey, come over here and sit on these blankets. I want to have a closer look at that vest." Now stunned, I picked my way around her display and sat down next to her.

The woman never introduced herself. And she was very direct in speaking to me. I took off my vest and handed it to her so she could look at my workmanship. She took her time in going over all the details. Finally, as she handed the vest back to me she said, "Your craftsmanship is as good as ours. We should do business together."

I nearly fell off the blanket pile and struggled to maintain my composure as I asked, "Just what kind of business do you have in mind?" Without hesitation, the artist pushed on, "We need special clothing for our Feast Day celebrations and you could make them for us. We want our own Santo Domingo designs that could be silk-screened from pottery, jewelry, and blanket designs. We could trade for goods."

It took me a while to absorb what the woman was proposing. And then I said, "The problem is, we live in California and I'm not sure how easy it would be to work out a business relationship with you." Once again, without hesitation, my new friend said, "You need to move here. We need to do business." Other women began to take notice of my vest and conversation with their neighbor, as they ambled over for a closer look. When Mike found me, I was in the midst of a group of Native women. We were talking a mile a minute and having a great time negotiating a business deal.

Me and My Magical Life

As Mike stood with wide eyes and a big grin, I was busy making a list of orders for ceremonial clothing. When I left my blanket perch, I had five hundred dollars in orders, with sketches of design ideas and an agreement to deliver the finished products the following year. I was instructed to pick out a few pieces of jewelry as a down payment. My stunned and amused spouse suggested we have a margarita and ponder what had just transpired. We headed off to La Fonda where, over drinks, we replayed the scene that had just taken place. Mike said he would never forget approaching the portal and seeing his wife sitting on a pile of blankets in the midst of a group of Native women artists, transacting a business deal.

And that was when we decided to pack up and move to New Mexico. Shortly after we returned to Eureka, I was summoned to a staff meeting at the senior center. It was there I planned to announce that Mike and I had decided to give up our ideal life and move to a little Spanish village in Northern New Mexico.

I had a paper grocery bag with a lot of turquoise and silver Indian jewelry that I had collected as down payment from my new Santo Domingo Pueblo friends. I took it to the meeting and promptly dumped it out on the big conference table in front of the entire staff. A gasp went up around the table because it was an impressive sight.

And then everybody spoke at once, horrified yet intrigued by my announcement. My coworkers had a hard time imagining that Mike and I could just walk away from seven and a half years of hard work putting together a successful business for Mike and a dynamic career for me.

Sitting at that table in front of a pile of turquoise and silver jewelry, I knew that our fate was to be in the land where the jewelry had been made by Native hands. I told everyone that Mike and I wanted the opportunity to make our own furniture, build with adobe, and generally create everything we would need for a new life. Most of all we wanted to own property, because we were aware of what we were capable of making out of virtually nothing. And we were tired of doing it for someone else.

Mike and I were proud of our accomplishments during our time in Eureka, and we remembered what our wealthy retired industrialist friend told us before we left Mexico. During dinner one night with my psychology teacher and her husband, we were given some sage advice. The husband had said, "Always quit while you are at the top of your game and about to take on a new challenge. You must use your past success as the reminder of what you are capable of in the new venture." Our friend was a wise and successful man and we trusted his advice. It has served us well.

During the drive back to California, Mike and I mapped out a plan for the next year and a half. I had a grant to complete and Mike had a business to run, but we put out word that Promotional Arts was for sale. That alone set things in motion: we had several interested buyers so we had to come up with a price. Our accountant and lawyer helped work that out, and sooner than we imagined, we had a sale. The buyer had no printing experience and asked that Mike mentor him for several months. That gave us time to get the rest of our life in order.

Living in a twelve-room flat, we had accumulated a lot of treasures from St. Vincent de Paul thrift store. We wound up having a household sale in half of Mike's store and sold six thousand dollars in goods before it was over. In a way, it was shocking to empty our share of the

Me and My Magical Life

household items in our flat. We had transformed that former brothel into a vibrant living space that we treasured.

From that point on, life was a blur. Between the getaway place, Mike's business, and the flat, we had a lot to undo. And all the goodbyes that went on for weeks. And the 1962 cattle truck that we bought from our rancher landlord to be transformed into a moving van. If that seemed farfetched, the idea of arriving in Chacon, New Mexico, with a commercial moving van seemed even more so. We also thought we would save money. We didn't, by a long shot. That trip was a nightmare that went on for weeks. But it did provide a lot of laughs in the end, and the beginning of my first book. You will have to read Accidental Anthropologists for that story.

27
New Mexico Bound

It took until November of 1983 to get our show on the road. Not exactly the best time of the year to be heading to high mountains, but after all our loose ends were tied there was no reason to linger. Once we made the decision we couldn't wait to get started creating a new life. We sold most of my household furnishings from my former marriage with the idea that we wanted to create our own to fit within the new surroundings. Whatever that meant!

We sold Promotional Arts for enough money to live carefully for a couple of years and for a down payment on a piece of property. It was a luxury we could never have imagined a few years before, and it made us think once again about our friend's advice about leaving at the top of your game. Chacon was our choice for a place to live, at least for a while. The narrow valley was so isolated that without an income we couldn't have survived. The pull was the solitude and the fact that we had good friends. Over the years, the Abeyta family had become an extension of ours, and they were thrilled to have us back, especially as a couple. Mike and I still had a lot of contacts in Chacon, so it was easy enough to rent a place.

We were fortunate to find the Presbyterian teacher's house available. It was at the end of the paved county road, next door to the church. The community center was across the road. Our new home had eight rooms, a six-foot bathtub, a long covered front porch, a patio with a river rock barbecue, and a lovely little back yard. The rent was one hundred and fifty dollars a month. And it was furnished, a bonus because our broken-down cattle truck/moving van was waiting it out until spring in the Dwelley barn. We were in heaven-and toasted one another with champagne during a huge snowstorm on our first day, December 15.

Shortly after New Year's Day a huge blizzard closed the roads for several days. We had been invited to a party in Las Vegas and when we got ready to leave, Mike went out to turn the car around and warm it up. We couldn't see the road from the house and once he faced the little highway around the curve he was stunned to see a guy on a horse plowing through three feet of snow. Mike ran in to give me the news, and I quickly called Bessie for confirmation and was horrified to hear they had seven-foot drifts up against their house.

I was all dressed up, standing in the doorway, when Mike came back in, and I started to fall apart. All of a sudden, it wasn't just the isolation that hit me. It was the realization that we had uprooted ourselves from a secure world and set ourselves down in the middle of nowhere, with no way out for days. I started to cry and then howl with great racking sobs. I began to shout at Mike, "How could you let me talk you into this? Why didn't you stop me?" All the while knowing it was my idea in the first place. And then Mike was shouting at me, asking the same questions. There we stood, dressed in party attire, accusing one another of destroying our lives by making stupid decisions based on answers from the wind!

The shouting went on for a while, until we realized we were stuck together in deep snow with no way out.

Me and My Magical Life

The Las Vegas newspaper was delivered to our post office box, and there was a recent issue on the table. Through swollen eyes I read that a space launch was to take place in Florida the following week. I turned to Mike and said, "We need to get out of here for a while. Let's drive to Cape Canaveral and watch the rocket launch." Now, I'm asking the same guy I just yelled at to drive me all the way to Florida in the dead of winter to watch a rocket blast off. Without hesitation, Mike heartily agreed. And that was a perfect example of our life together; Mike always told people that I am the artistic director and he is the set designer, even if we disagree at times.

As soon as the road was clear we drove our little yellow Honda hard for three days to get to the launch in time. In fact, we made it just hours before the launch. We were directed to a parking area where thousands of people were already assembled. It was three thirty a.m. and somehow we slept sitting up, and I was surprised to awaken to the smell of coffee. A pleasant man was walking among the vehicles, selling cups of coffee, and he revived us. We saw a lot of motor homes with American flags flying, and people lined the edge of the bay for a good view of the liftoff. Mike and I joined the crowd and entered into the thrill and excitement of the moment. It was a perfect launch and an experience to be remembered.

We spent a couple of days in a motel on the beach and then toured Florida from one coast to the other and on to the Panhandle.

We had an old friend from Mexico days who lived in Pensacola, so we headed in that direction. We had stayed in touch with Mark Price and wound up spending three days with him at his beachfront home on stilts. Heading toward Texas, Mike and I discussed dropping in unannounced on other old friends, something we knew they would get a kick out of. We did just that, arriving at their door in Houston on an overcast Saturday afternoon. Sheldon and Mary Ann Tucker were delighted to see us, but we were even more surprised, because they were about to have a wedding for their son Craig and his fiancée.

Mike and I were embarrassed that we had crashed the wedding, but Mary Ann said, "This is perfectly timed. I'm much too nervous to deal with Joyce and her family so Charlotte, you can take charge." And that is what I did. The Tuckers are sixty-year friends and I had always been close to the children, so it was a great opportunity to catch up with all of them at once. And they had a huge house with room for everyone.

By the time Mike and I returned from our southern tour, the weather had warmed a bit and we had mellowed out. The trip gave us time to think about our new life, and we soon jumped into a big Halley's Comet T-shirt and poster project that would go on for over a year. That project also launched Mike's new T-shirt printing business: Pajarito Graphics. That year I painted a three-panel, folding screen with life-size hollyhocks, inspired by the flowers that lined our front porch. And another inspiration came out of a Newsweek magazine article that led to a set of kitchen chairs, and a great story.

It was in that remote place that I launched my clothing line in earnest. Having access to Taos, Las Vegas, and Santa Fe opened new possibilities for us both. Mike and I were about to enter into a business opportunity and lasting friendship in a most unlikely place. Fortunately for us we had Las Vegas friends from years past, so it was quite easy to fall back into a social life. It was also helpful in getting the word out about Mike's printing business.

Me and My Magical Life

A business friend introduced us to Andrew Maclehose, the man I had heard about at the Steins' bookstore and the dean at the new Armand Hammer United World College of the American Southwest. The school was about to sponsor a 5K run for faculty and students, and Andrew wanted T-shirts for participants. Mike and I drove out to the college in our little pickup truck that was covered in moss and rust.

After meeting with Andrew and working out details, the dean accompanied us to our truck. We stood talking for a while and as we turned to leave, Andrew said goodbye at the same time he smacked his hand down on the truck fender. A rain of moss and rust flew off. The poor dean was horrified by what he had unleashed, but Mike and I were laughing out loud. We quickly told Andrew about our adventurous move and added that we had always had a reputation as eccentric.

The next time we met outside the dean's office I was wearing a colorful ensemble that was sure to draw attention, and Andrew noticed. After taking care of business details Andrew asked us to sit beneath an apple tree so we could chat. He offered to put us up in the castle during the two-day 5K run event, but we declined his generosity because we loved driving to and from Chacon and sleeping in our own bed.

Mike proposed setting up a portable silk screen on campus during the event to print shirts on demand. That way, the school wouldn't have to pay for unused shirts. Andrew, being Scottish, appreciated the gesture, which endeared us to him. As we were departing that time, Andrew made it a point to tell us that Brits most always have a soft spot for eccentrics.

From that time on, Andrew took it upon himself to involve us in as many school activities as possible.

Charlotte Plantz

We were invited to concerts, lectures, and anything else of interest at the school. One evening Mike and I attended a lecture that Andrew was giving. At the conclusion, the two of us were standing outside the door with a group of Las Vegas friends when Andrew approached us. He said he and his wife would like for us to join them for a drink at their home. Everyone was watching as we thanked him and said we would be right down.

Andrew headed down the hill and we found ourselves chatting longer than anticipated. A little while later Andrew suddenly appeared in front of us and said, "I meant now!" Not in a spiteful way, but in the way of a headmaster. However, it did elicit a drawing in of breath from the group around us. It was the beginning of a great friendship with the dean and his wife, but it put Mike and me in a spotlight that soon became uncomfortable with our old friends.

Mike and I did join Andrew and Heather for drinks. It was our first introduction to Heather, and the three of us hit it off immediately. We also met the three Maclehose daughters: Laura, Rachel, and Harriet. Laura was in high school, Rachel in middle school, and Harriet in third grade. As we grew to know the girls it became apparent that Harriet and I shared a fondness for fashions with flair. The child wore stylish hats and exotic outfits to school so no wonder her dad noticed my out-of-the-ordinary wardrobe.

As it turned out, Heather became my partner in the clothing line I had going with the Santo Domingo Pueblo artists. Heather did most of the sewing and accompanied me on deliveries to the Pueblo. The first time we parked in front of the little Pueblo store, before we even got out of the car, a line of artists had assembled next to the car. While Heather and I were unloading clothing from the trunk, jewelry and pottery appeared from beneath the artists' blankets. The transaction took place so quickly it had the two of us spinning in our tracks.

Cash was never involved. All of our business was done with trade of goods. By the time our venture ran its course, the two of us had amassed piles of silver and turquoise jewelry, several pairs of moccasins, and a few painted ceramic pots. Andrew thought us quite mad for not making any money. But he did humor us. And his daughters enjoyed playing with all that jewelry.

Most frontier towns have a code of behavior among inhabitants that prohibits grandstanding. You must never stand out or draw attention to yourself. If anyone else causes that to happen, it becomes your fault. Andrew was so outgoing and dynamic he couldn't help but put us in the spotlight every time we were in public. When Mike and I entered a concert hall Andrew would jump up and shout our names, then lead us to the front row to join him and Heather. We could see students and teachers staring at us as they tried to figure out who we were and where we came from. I spoke to Andrew about it but he just laughed and went right on with his greetings.

Our friendship with the dean and his family saw us through some tough financial times after we bought our place March 1st,1985. By 1986 we had spent our financial cushion. Had it not been for money that we had set aside for house payments we probably would have lost our home. I could afford to buy only one bar of soap at a time, and that pretty much applied to everything we needed to survive.

One day after a lunatic neighbor shut off our water for four days, I drove to the college for a shower at the Maclehoses'. When Andrew asked how things were going, I burst into tears. I said I was holding our life together with nothing but sheer will. I really wailed when he said, "That's right. You are holding it together with nothing but willpower and a lot of hard work." That was entirely true, because Mike was working his butt off growing his silk-screen business.

Andrew and Heather would call to say they were going to pick us up for an outing or to invite us to a meal. Just as the college was going on spring break, Andrew called to tell us that we were going to accompany the family and ten students on a five-day canoe trip down the Rio Grande at Big Bend National Park. When I objected because we had not a cent, the dean said, "Be ready by eight a.m. on Friday and we'll pick you up." I argued that I had never been in a canoe and was terrified of water. His response, "See you on Friday."

That turned out to be the trip of a lifetime. Shortly before we put into the water, a canoe broke in half, but Mike and Andrew saved the day by using a roll of duct tape. That canoe held through rapids to the end of the trip. Mike and I capsized on the last day in a sizeable rapid, and I popped up laughing as I swam to shore. The water was warm, our belongings were wrapped in plastic, and there were thirteen people standing by to rescue us. I lost my fear of canoe trips that day.

Mike and I spent four wonderful years with the Maclehose family and the United World College. We became a getaway family that hosted a slew of foreign students and their families. The Berlin Wall came down just after Mike printed a T-shirt designed by a German student that featured a flower from each side of the wall intertwined in a hole in the wall. We hosted a Polish family with a dad who had been a friend of Lech Walesa before the fall of the Iron Curtain. A wonderful woman from Nepal stayed with us during her daughter's graduation and informed me that she thought we had been connected in a previous life. She also said our village reminded her of their home in a village outside Kathmandu, the landscapes being similar.

There we were, in the middle of nowhere, with exotic folks showing up on a regular basis. Andrew delighted in bringing foreign visitors from the airport to tour our adobe ruin. From the kitchen window I would be horrified to see a van filled with Italians or Japanese pouring out the side doors, cameras snapping away. When I scolded him he always said he was proud to share our vision. It was his belief that gave us courage to keep plowing ahead, and it sustained us during their time in New Mexico.

Mike and I were not finished with the Maclehose family after they moved to a series of countries before settling in their old stone farmhouse in Wales. We visited them when they lived in Switzerland and Andrew was headmaster at the Geneva International School's English Division. Our friends took us on a nine-day whirlwind car tour of Italy, Slovenia, and Croatia. Venice was a highlight, but so were Pula and the island of Cres in Croatia while war raged in Yugoslavia across the Adriatic Sea.

We camped every night in splendid campgrounds and did not have to visit refugee camps that had been on the agenda because the refugees had been assimilated into the local populations. We spent an evening having dinner in a Croatian family's courtyard that had been turned into a restaurant. Shortly after we arrived, the owner picked up his accordion and played "Oh! Susanna," the only American song he knew. We had a good laugh when I informed him that had been our wedding song in Mexico for the same reason. A group of five young fishermen joined us and wound up entertaining us until midnight after the owner handed them an accordion and carafe of wine. In perfect harmony, the group sang Russian and Croatian folk songs that held us spellbound.

Over the years, various members of the Maclehose clan stayed with us on occasions. It was always a great way to bond with the Maclehose daughters. We visited the family a couple of times in Wales and remain close. Mike and I will always be grateful to Armand Hammer for choosing Montezuma Castle and Las Vegas for the only school of its kind in the United States. And we are grateful to Andrew and Heather for including us in their world.

Not long after Heather and Andrew moved to Europe, we were introduced to a fascinating woman named Gwendolyn, who called herself a cowboy. Our old friend, Barry, was starting a newspaper business in Cimarron and brought Gwendolyn to meet us. He knew we would hit it off.

I called her Gwendolyn the Cowboy from the very beginning for, it was apparent she was no ordinary cowgirl despite her outward appearance. Gwendolyn was waif-like, not as tiny as Edith Piaf, who happened to be one of her favorite singers, but small nevertheless. She had two prominent features: the wild mane of hair that fell down her back nearly to her waist and her eyes. I have never met anyone who had eyes like hers. They actually crackled and sparked as she began to speak. Gwendolyn was animated when she spoke, hands gesturing wildly as though punctuating sentences as words tumbled out of her mouth. Without a doubt, she was the most captivating woman I had ever met. It was great fun having a conversation with her, and we connected almost immediately.

Me and My Magical Life

It was a long drive to Cimarron, so it took a while before I drove up to visit. She lived on a medium size ranch belonging to a family of local ranchers. She lived there alone, protected by 3 blue heelers who would have made mincemeat of an intruder. The dogs had the run of a small fenced-in yard, so my friend felt secure in her Shangri-la. Eight screeching peacocks and hens roamed the ranch yards, giving the place an exotic touch. A greenhouse was attached to the front porch, where Gwendolyn tended a veritable jungle of greenery. On Sundays, she hosted champagne brunches and croquet games for neighboring girlfriends.

Gwendolyn was one of the most adventurous women I had met in a long time. She made her living breaking and training workhorses, and worked as a wrangler during roundups and brandings. A painting of her done by a friend, showed her astride her favorite mare, plunging almost vertically down an embankment during a roundup. Her favorite sport was barrel-racing during rodeo season and I think dudes in the stands must have been swooning out of the bleachers. Gwendolyn was about to turn fifty and I was pretty sure she would never turn matronly!

The next time I saw Gwendolyn, Mike was with me. That summer was one of the hottest on record for the area. The temps soared to 104 and hung there for days. We always had wind or at least a breeze, but not that summer. Not a leaf stirred. Grasshoppers were eating everything in their path. I was born in Kansas on a day exactly like that. My father removed windows and hung wet blankets in them to help cool my poor mother and newborn me. I wondered whether we should follow suit. But instead, we decided to head north in search of coolness. It was Fourth of July weekend and we stopped to see

Charlotte Plantz

Gwendolyn and get advice on the highest, coolest place in the area. She talked us into spending the night with her, even though her outdoor thermometer read 105. We were too hot to protest.

During that visit Gwendolyn told us a story about playing Frisbee with the moon! She said she had returned from a three-day roundup, hot, tired, and aching, but, still restless and full of energy. It was just beginning to get dark when she showered and put on a pale blue dotted-Swiss cotton dress. The restless cowboy looked around for shoes, and the only thing she saw was a pair of cowboy boots, so she put those on and grabbed a Frisbee on her way out the door. Gwendolyn, had no idea what she wanted to do with all that energy so she walked out to a front pasture where seven, 2000 lb bulls were grazing. The woman had no fear whatsoever of those animals, or anything else. Through the trees, a full moon suddenly appeared. Gwendolyn was so struck by the sight she started throwing the Frisbee into a stiff breeze that had come up just as quickly. So there she was: Gwendolyn the cowboy, knee deep in bull patties, wearing a blue dress and cowboy boots, playing Frisbee with the moon!

From the time I heard the story I couldn't get the image out of my head. It simply wouldn't go away. One day I awoke, ate my breakfast, and marched out to my studio, where I started tearing painted paper into little pieces. I had been trying to figure out how to recreate that scene for weeks, and that morning it all came together. I had the beginning of a collage of Gwendolyn the Cowboy playing Frisbee with the moon.

I made a special trip to Gwendolyn's ranch for the sole purpose of drawing the bulls and recreating the scene in the pasture. From then on, the collage created itself, and I knew I had something special. So special it sold

Me and My Magical Life

immediately to a couple in Colorado, but not before Mike had time to reproduce 3 poster size copies on a new large format copy machine at the print shop.

I carried a copy to Gwendolyn, who was amazed that I could create a piece of art out of her simple story. I handed her the poster and she stood looking at it for a while. Without saying a word, she went to her bedroom. When she returned, she was holding a pair of red snakeskin cowboy boots. We both gasped, because in the collage, I had given the cowboy a pair of torn red paper 'snakeskin' cowboy boots. Gwendolyn had never mentioned what color boots she was wearing during her Frisbee game. We took it as a sign of more magic in our lives.

Several years later, I was sad to see Gwendolyn leave Cimarron and head for Utah, another of her favorite places. Mike and I saw her five years later in Escalante. Her eyes still flashed. She was still attractive and had all her animals. The woman read all the New York Times best seller books, taught herself French, and attracted high-level men who always led to trouble. It wouldn't be long before she left that little town and we never saw her again. But I will never forget Gwendolyn or her stories. And we have a poster to remind us of those red cowboy boots.

28
At Last, A Place of Our Own

When the opportunity to buy a house came up in 1985, I reluctantly agreed to take a look. Our life in Chacon was so peaceful and quiet it was hard to think about changing it. Realistically, our nest egg had dwindled so it was time to get serious about making a living. We had been driving hundreds of miles doing business in the three small cities, and the time involved had become ridiculous so that pushed us into making a decision.

The property included a small one-hundred-year-old adobe house and an outbuilding ruin sitting on top of a one-acre mesita overlooking the river. The outside walls of the house were badly eroded and the rusted steel roof sported a bullet-hole-riddled chamber pot turned upside down over a vent pipe. Had it not been for the interior of the little house we might not have bought it. However, the inside had been lovingly renovated, and the sunken bathtub won us over.

The magnificent view played a large part as well: after living in small sky country among the Pacific Coast redwoods, the wide-open vista took our breath away. Without speaking, Mike and I saw the potential for our boundless energy and made the leap. It took a lot of years, but we managed to realize every fantasy we ever had. Along the way, people gave us two houses: one adobe and the other a 1936 Sears Roebuck kit house that we dismantled and rebuilt.

Mike and I designed an adobe casita and sunroom, and he and a young friend built it from scratch. A neighbor built our garage. I designed our kitchen chairs, which eventually sparked another memorable event. The chairs had been designed and made while we lived in Chacon. I had seen a Newsweek article about an architect named Robert Venturi with a picture of whimsical chairs that he had designed. I fell in love with them and took designs that I had cut out of newspaper to an eighty-four-year-old local furniture maker of some renown. Eusebio Vasquez laughed at my proposal, saying he was known for his classical Spanish furniture. But he would think about it. After giving the idea some thought, Eusebio decided he would like the challenge and built six chairs in three different designs. He informed me he had used one hundred twenty wooden pegs in each chair for durability. And he made me promise that I would never tell anybody that he had made the chairs. He said he had his reputation to protect.

And that made me think about knocking off Robert Venturi's chair designs. As an artist, I hated that idea. A number of amazing events took place after we moved to our new home, and one of those occurred when an architect friend brought his visiting architect friend from Maine to dinner.

The minute Rock stepped into our kitchen, he nearly shouted, " OMG, those chairs. Where did you get those chairs?" My heart began to race and my face turned red, as I stammered, "I copied them from Robert Venturi, and I have always been afraid of getting busted." Our guest started to laugh, and went on, "I worked as an intern for Venturi during his whimsical chair period.

Me and My Magical Life

They were all over the workspace, and we kept tripping over the ridiculous legs that stuck out." I didn't know whether to laugh or cry. But I did begin to calm down as he went on, "Venturi would love what you did with your chairs; they are much more practical and beautifully crafted. I can tell you, he would be pleased to have inspired you."

29
Some Extraordinary Events

Five months after we had settled in, we had a phone call from Pat, our friend Murray's partner when they lived in Taos. Mike and I had stayed with them on our honeymoon. Pat and Murray had shared a love of photography and had spent time the following year driving around the state shooting pictures of old abandoned adobes. Pat said she had a friend who lived near us and she would be visiting him the following week.

Pat lived in Santa Fe and had just found out about us from a mutual Montana friend. She came to see us before her date with our neighbor. When I opened the door, Pat was as white as a sheet. I asked if she was okay and she said, "No, I need to sit down." We offered her a chair and a glass of water. None of us had recovered from Murray's suicide four years earlier, so Pat's visit was emotional. The brilliant young man's loss was still unbearable for us all.

The three of us sat at the kitchen table silently, feeling Murray's presence until Pat said, "You won't believe what I'm about to tell you. Murray and I photographed this very house in June of 1975. It was a ruin then. I'm not sure how we stumbled on it, but we were taken with the view and setting and took lots of pictures."

Charlotte Plantz

Pat went on, "Murray and I spent a long time sitting on your mesita talking about life and our futures. And here is the strange and amazing thing that Murray said to me. He said, 'I love it here. This is where I want to live. Right here in this adobe ruin." No one could speak for a while and I couldn't stop crying. Mike and I had bought the property March 1st and moved in on June 1, 1985. The shock was so profound none of us has ever forgotten that evening.

With Pat's story still fresh in our minds, soon Mike and I experienced another extraordinary event. This one had to do with a roadrunner, the New Mexico State Bird, and me. It began in my flower garden outside the kitchen. It was late summer and I had cosmos all around the house. It was the one flower you could count on in this harsh place. I had planted cosmos seeds the first year we moved here, and they had reseeded themselves until the drought began in earnest. 1991 may have been one of the best cosmos years to date; there were masses of them all around the yard.

One afternoon I walked out to pick a bouquet. As I approached the blooming mass facing the mesa, a large roadrunner sprang out of the flowers. I nearly jumped out of my skin. We stood staring at one another with not more than three feet separating us. Neither of us moved as I said, "Well, well, well, what a surprise seeing you here. I see you are enjoying my flowers." The bird never took its eyes off me until it turned and slowly walked away. It was the most wonderful experience, and I could hardly wait to share my tale with Mike.

The next day I was sitting at the kitchen table having lunch, as always reading Newsweek while I slowly chewed. My head jerked up as I thought I saw something go by the window in the door. And then I

Me and My Magical Life

heard a thump outside the door. Curiosity got the better of me and I got up to peer out. Below me, just in front of the door, stood the roadrunner, looking up at me. The bird had literally jumped up to see in the window. The sound I had heard was its fall to the ground. What I had seen was the bird flashing past the window. The roadrunner turned around several times and then stopped to look up at me again. I could hardly believe my eyes as it walked slowly across the yard toward the arroyo.

I ran to the telephone, dialed the print shop, and breathlessly awaited my husband's voice. Mike had gone to work at the Highlands University print shop in June of 1990, and continued printing T-shirts at night for another two years. I knew I could count on Mike to give me an honest answer, so it was vital for me to tell him my story and get his reaction. As usual, his response was, "Wow, far out." He almost always says that in spite of the fact that the expression went out of style at least forty years ago. But that was one of the reasons I loved him; he never seemed to notice changing fashions, automobile styles, music, and certainly never expressions. Mike did add, "What an incredible experience for you both." He did not tease me, laugh at me, or in any way diminish my enthusiasm. He also believed my story.

When I went for the mail I told Trini, the postmaster, about my experience. He grew quiet and serious as he said to me, "Charlotte, if this had happened here fifty years ago, people would say that bird was someone who had died and was trying to make contact with you. The roadrunner has always been a special bird here, and it has a magical quality about it. You are very lucky to have such an experience. It means something." I was so relieved to hear Trini's reaction, especially the fact that he believed my tale. I could hardly believe it myself.

Charlotte Plantz

Thursday night we had an overnight visitor, a friend passing through on his way back from Colorado. Joel was someone who could understand the entire roadrunner experience for what it was. He did not think me deranged in the least. Joel drove off the next morning, and I went out to my studio and the guest room upstairs. As I came down the stairs with my arms full of sheets, my head jerked up when I saw the roadrunner perching on a narrow ledge outside the west window, directly across the room from me.

I dropped the sheets and walked in a daze to the window. The bird didn't move and we locked eyes as I said, "Who are you and what do you want with me?" It stared through the glass at me and then turned its head slowly to look out at the landscape. I pulled my drawing stool over in front of the window, climbed on, and there we sat-eye to eye, as I began to draw the magnificent bird.

Each time the roadrunner turned its head toward me all the feathers around its neck fluffed up, displaying a lovely shade of orange just beneath the darker top layer. We sat like that for at least fifteen minutes. I was mesmerized as it continued to swing its head slowly around from me to the landscape and back again. I could not move, nor did I want to because I did not want the experience to end. Who but Mike and Trini would believe this? After I told the two of them about that episode I felt like a fool for not believing it to be a very special event in my life. Though for the life of me I could not imagine who among the deceased might be trying to get my attention. Oddly, I didn't think about Murray because Trini had told me that a bird usually showed up shortly after a loved ones death.

I did not see the roadrunner for a few days, and I must admit as each day passed I felt a sense of

Me and My Magical Life

disappointment when it did not turn up. Just when I thought it had all been a figment of my imagination, the bird would show up again, sometimes outdoors where I worked in the yard. On those occasions the roadrunner merely stayed nearby catching grasshoppers as I continued with my chore.

During one more lunch in the kitchen the roadrunner came to call. I had my back to the kitchen sink window, nose in my magazine, when I heard the tiniest sound. Even before I turned around I knew the roadrunner was there. Sure enough, there it stood on the wide window ledge, peering in at me. That time I laughed and called out, "Who are you? What are you trying to tell me?" The majestic bird merely stared at me for a moment and then jumped back to earth and sauntered away.

A few days later a friend dropped by and I decided to tell him my roadrunner story. Douglas listened politely without interrupting, and then he said, "Charlotte, I've known you a long time, this is very hard to believe, but I know you as a no-nonsense woman, very grounded. There is no reason to believe you would make this story up." We had a cup of tea and then I walked him out to his truck. At the same moment, we saw the roadrunner coming up the driveway, oblivious to the stranger, on a direct course for the truck.

The bird jumped up on the hood of the truck and did its turning, staring routine right in front of us both. Our mouths flew open simultaneously as we stood paralyzed. The bird took its time, finally jumping down for a slow and steady retreat. Finally Douglas said, "I cannot believe what I just experienced. I tried to believe your story but it was hard. And now the roadrunner has come to make me a believer."

Charlotte Plantz

Every day for weeks I watched for the bird, always longing for a sign or answer to the why of it all. The roadrunner stayed in the area through November and December. I would see it cross the driveway down by the gate or run across the yard chasing grasshoppers until the first major freeze of winter. The roadrunner never came near me again, and I continued to wonder about that bird in my life as winter wore on. One early morning Mike and I were preparing breakfast together. Suddenly Mike turned to me saying, "You know, I think that roadrunner is your ex-husband trying to make contact with you." I shivered, not wanting that connection with the majestic bird.

Just then, I went to turn on National Public Radio, a regular morning program for us. They were giving a national weather report and the announcer said, "Tropical Storm Fabian is heading up the coast of North Carolina." I whirled around to see the look of astonishment on my husband's face. Our mouths flew open, eyes huge as we both spoke at once. The timing was incredible, given the fact that my ex-husband's name was Fabian, rather an unusual name and rarely heard.

Mike laughed, saying, "If that isn't a sign I don't know what is." From that day on I couldn't shake off the feeling that Mike may have been right. I had been so full of anger I had totally repressed my former marriage of eighteen years. If it hadn't been for my daughters I would probably never have thought about the man again.

I do not know why I had not thought of the connection before then. Fabian had died of a heart attack the previous August. Trini had told me that the roadrunner represented someone who had died, someone who wanted to make contact with me. In New Mexico, grief counseling may include stories about birds being

Me and My Magical Life

conduits to loved ones from the deceased, So, from that day on I could not stop thinking about my former husband and my life with him. Eighteen years was a long time and there had to have been some good parts of that life. I thought about my daughters and how loving and funny they are. Their father was a devoted father, very loving. And he was funny. He told great stories and always made people laugh.

When our daughters were young Fabian would delight the neighbor children with all sorts of fantastical high jinks such as the worm catching device he put together after a rainstorm. He placed two large screwdrivers in the ground and hooked a wire between them to a battery. I don't remember what he used to generate a shock, but when he did, huge numbers of earthworms jumped right up out of the ground. The children would shriek with delight as they ran up and down the wire grabbing those poor stunned worms.

Fabian had been an avid fisherman and a clever one at that; fresh fish had been a constant in our diet. I wondered more and more about my anger and blocked-out previous life. It was true that my husband had been unfaithful and had led a double life, but my blocking him out went beyond that. It had to do with my own forgiveness and letting go of that chapter. Once I had the insight into what was going on inside my own head, a most amazing event took place.

About a week after Tropical Storm Fabian headed up the coast of North Carolina from Bermuda, Mike and I had finished dinner and he had gone out to his shop to print T-shirts. I stayed inside to wash dishes and ponder the roadrunner connection. My mind began to race over all the thoughts I had been having the past few weeks regarding my ex-husband, and the pros and cons of our life together. Julie and Cyndi kept popping into my head, with all their best attributes at the surface of my awareness. Cyndi looked the most like her father and certainly had his sense of fun and humor. Julie was a great storyteller, always entertaining, making people laugh. Both women are a delight to be with.

The more I thought about my daughters, the more credit I had to give their father. The more I was able to do that, the more positive things began to surface. Pretty soon it was like a wellspring; nothing but loving thoughts taking me back over my life. If it had not been for my life with the Minnesota Dutch-German farm boy, I would not be who I am and I would never have had my wonderful daughters.

As all of those thoughts whirled around inside my head, I stood at the sink with my hands immersed in suds and began to cry. The cry turned into sobs and I couldn't stop, nor did I want to; the feeling of relief was immense. In the midst of my sobs a vision appeared in the form of a huge heart. The heart rose up out of the dish suds in front of my eyes, hanging there for a while, pulsating goodness and love. The feelings wrapped around me, releasing me from all the bitterness I had been holding in for all those years. It was a heart of forgiveness and I knew in a flash that the roadrunner had been its messenger.

A year or so after the magic encounters with the roadrunner, I did a series of drawings depicting the most notable events and then wrote the story. A couple of years later when our grandsons were here for the summer, I decided to share the drawings and story with them. Mike insisted I tell them the whole story, including the "goodness of Grandpa Babe's heart." As a teenager he was nicknamed after Babe Ruth because of the physical resemblance they shared. Alex was four years old, Tyler

Me and My Magical Life

seven, and Andrew eight. We all slept in my studio, with Mike and me upstairs and the children in the double daybed downstairs. Every night when the boys were tucked in I read them a story. That night I shared the drawings as I related the tale.

The three of them sat up to see the pictures better and were amazed that I had actually drawn them. It was probably their first awareness that their granny was an artist. Their eyes grew huge as I went on with the story and realized myself what a magical tale it was for my grandsons. I glossed over the anger part and got right to the part about Grandpa Babe's heart coming up out of the soapsuds. As I finished, I looked at the children, their faces full of amazement. Andrew had tears running down his cheeks. He was quiet for a moment and then spoke, "Oh Granny, I wish I had been here to see the goodness of Grandpa Babe's heart."

Remembering Pat's story about Murray wanting to live in this exact place brought it all full circle for me. The life that I had to let go of all those years before had freed me to create another that wound up having all the best elements of the past.

"At the moment when you are most confused about what you should do with your life, the smartest bet is to do what millions of men and women have done through history. Pick yourself up and go out alone into the wilderness."

David Brooks-

"The Second Mountain"

Made in the
USA
Lexington, KY